ICFA Continuing Education
Investing in Small-Cap and Microcap Securities

Proceedings of the AIMR seminar *Investing in and the Portfolio Management of Small-Cap and Microcap Securities*

September 25, 1996
Boston, Massachusetts

John C. Bogle, Jr., CFA
David B. Breed, CFA
Daniel N. Ginsparg
Daniel L. Jacobs, CFA
William D.B. Koenig, CFA

Claudia E. Mott, *Moderator*
Thomas V. Reilly, CFA
Marc R. Reinganum
Peter C. Schliemann

To obtain the *AIMR Publications Catalog*, contact:
AIMR, P.O. Box 3668, Charlottesville, Virginia 22903, U.S.A.
Phone 804-980-3668; Fax 804-980-9755; E-mail info@aimr.org
or
visit AIMR's World Wide Web site at **www.aimr.org**
to view the AIMR publications list.

ICFA Continuing Education is published monthly seven times a year in March, March, April, May, July, September, and November by the Association for Investment Management and Research, P.O. Box 3668, Charlottesville, Virginia 22903, U.S.A. This publication is designed to provide accurate and authoritative information with regard to the subject matter covered. It is sold with the understanding that the publisher is not engaged in rendering legal, accounting, or other professional services. If legal advice or other expert assistance is required, the services of a competent professional should be sought. Periodicals postage paid at the post office in Richmond, Virginia, and additional mailing offices.

Copies are mailed as a benefit of membership to CFA® charterholders. Subscriptions also are available at US$100 for one year. Address all circulation communications to ICFA Continuing Education, P.O. Box 3668, Charlottesville, Virginia 22903, U.S.A.; Phone 804-980-3668; Fax 804-980-9755. For change of address, send mailing label and new address six weeks in advance.

Postmaster: Send address changes to the Association for Investment Management and Research, P.O. Box 3668, Charlottesville, Virginia 22903.

ISBN 1-879087-81-2
Printed in the United States of America
March 1997

3 2280 00772 7852

Editorial Staff
Katrina F. Sherrerd, CFA
Senior Vice President

Charlene Semer
Editor

Jaynee M. Dudley
Production Manager

Marsha Gainey
Assistant Editor

Diane B. Hamshar
Typesetting/Layout

Contents

Foreword

This proceedings, the record of AIMR's seminar "Investing in and the Portfolio Management of Small-Cap and Microcap Securities," addresses a topic of growing interest among financial managers and their clients. The prospect of earning returns that substantially exceed those on conventional large-cap investments is certainly tempting, perhaps enough so to drown out warnings of greater risk with small-company securities. Some observers argue, however, that the validity of the "small-cap effect" is by no means certain. They point out that the outperformance of small-cap companies appears to be time specific, that the astounding gains those stocks made was limited to certain periods in the past, mainly from 1975 to 1983, when small-cap stocks returned an average of 35 percent a year. Perhaps the small-caps' outperformance during that nine-year period was sufficient to influence the overall historical data over a much longer period of time. This controversy will not soon be settled, and meanwhile the popularity of small-company investing continues to blossom.

The participants in this seminar are experienced in investing in small companies, and in this proceed-ings, they share their strategies and tools for weighing the pluses and minuses and reaching a balanced position on such investments. They are well equipped to advise newcomers and novices on how to know when to say yes and when to say no to a small-cap opportunity, when to buy in and when to exit this market. We are pleased to bring their insights to readers.

We would like to thank Claudia E. Mott of Prudential Securities for acting as moderator for this seminar. We would also like to thank the seminar's speakers for their valuable participation: John C. Bogle, Jr., CFA, Numeric Investors Limited Partnership; David B. Breed, CFA, Cadence Capital Management; Daniel N. Ginsparg, Boatmen's Trust Company; Daniel L. Jacobs, CFA, Jacobs Asset Management; William D.B. Koenig, CFA, Denro Fund Management Alberta; Thomas V. Reilly, CFA, Putnam Investment Management; Marc R. Reinganum, Southern Methodist University Finance Institute; and Peter C. Schliemann, David L. Babson & Company.

Katrina F. Sherrerd, CFA
Senior Vice President
Educational Products

Biographies of Speakers

John C. Bogle, Jr., CFA, is a partner in and the managing director of Numeric Investors Limited Partnership. His responsibilities include portfolio management of discretionary long, short, and hedged equity portfolios. Prior to joining Numeric, Mr. Bogle was the vice president of the Asset Management Division of State Street Bank and Trust Company. Mr. Bogle is a trustee of The Haverford School. He earned a B.A. and an M.B.A. from Vanderbilt University.

David B. Breed, CFA, cofounded Cadence Capital Management in 1988 and serves as CEO and chief investment officer. Mr. Breed also serves on the operating board of PIMCO Advisors, L.P. Prior to founding Cadence Capital Management, Mr. Breed served as a portfolio manager for Frontier Capital Management, an analyst and portfolio manager for Endowment Management and Research, and as an equity analyst at Loomis Sayles and Company. Mr. Breed received a B.A. in finance from the University of Massachusetts at Amherst and an M.B.A. from The Wharton School of Business.

Daniel N. Ginsparg works for Boatmen's Trust Company as senior portfolio manager for the small-cap and growth investment process. He is affiliated with the Saint Louis Society of Financial Analysts, the Chicago Quantitative Alliance, and the New York Society of Quantitative Analysts. Mr. Ginsparg received a B.S. in business administration and an M.B.A. in finance and operations research from the University of Missouri at St. Louis.

Daniel L. Jacobs, CFA, is the president and founder of Jacobs Asset Management. Previously, Mr. Jacobs spent more than 10 years at Templeton Investment Counsel, where he served as executive vice president and director. Prior to joining Templeton, he was a vice president and portfolio manager for the Institutional Investment Group and International Division of First National Bank of Atlanta. He is a founding member of the International Society of Financial Analysts. Mr. Jacobs received a B.A. in economics from Miami University and an M.B.A. in finance from Emory University.

William D.B. Koenig, CFA, serves as investment manager for Denro Fund Management Alberta, acting general manager of Data Trax Systems, treasurer for Steady State Automation, and director of Avatar Energy. Mr. Koenig's experience includes 12 years in the oil and gas sector, 2 years in the real estate sector, and 3 years in the financial sector. He currently serves on the Standards and Policy Subcommittee and the Candidate Curriculum Committee of AIMR. He is active in community involvement and has been recognized several times for his achievements by the Canadian Progress Club. Mr. Koenig received a B.C. in finance from the University of Calgary.

Claudia E. Mott is a first vice president and director of small-cap research for Prudential Securities. Ms. Mott was voted to *Institutional Investor* magazine's annual All-Star Research Team in each of the past five years, ranking first in the small-company category for the past three years. Prior to joining Prudential Securities, she was a senior consultant for Interactive Data Corporation and a financial analyst for Boston Gas Company. Ms. Mott received a B.B.A. degree from the University of Massachusetts at Amherst and an M.B.A. from Boston University.

Thomas V. Reilly, CFA, is managing director of Putnam Investment Management, where he serves the Value Equities Group as chief investment officer. He previously managed The George Putnam Fund of Boston, the Putnam Vista Fund, and the Putnam Convertible Income-Growth Trust. Prior to joining Putnam, Mr. Reilly worked for Massachusetts Mutual Insurance, Connecticut General Insurance, First Chicago Corporation, and Allstate Insurance. He has taught graduate-level courses in business administration at American International College and at Western New England College. Mr. Reilly received a B.A. from Knox College and an M.B.A. from the University of Chicago.

Marc R. Reinganum holds the Mary Jo Vaughn Rauscher Chair in Financial Investments and is the director of the Finance Institute at Southern Methodist University. Additionally, he serves as a consultant to major institutional investors. He is considered the founding father of stock market anomalies. Professor Reinganum received the Graham and Dodd Award for his research on small-cap stocks and has received national press coverage for his research on selecting superior securities. He has served on the editorial boards of numerous journals and continues to provide editorial review for several publications. Prior to joining the faculty at Southern Methodist University, he taught in the business schools at the University of Chicago, the University of Iowa, and the University of Southern California. Professor Reinganum earned an A.B. from Oberlin College and an M.B.A. and a Ph.D. from the University of Chicago.

Peter C. Schliemann serves as executive vice president and a member of the board of directors of David L. Babson & Company. He is also the head of Babson's small-company investment operations. He has been the manager of the Babson Enterprise Fund for more than 10 years and is comanager of the Babson Enterprise II Fund. Mr. Schliemann received an A.B. from Amherst College and an M.B.A. from Harvard University.

Investing in Small-Cap and Microcap Securities: An Overview

In many ways, investing in small-capitalization and microcapitalization companies is a gamble. The payoff for being right may be very handsome indeed, or there may be no payoff at all—even losses. To help reduce the element of chance, the speakers at AIMR's seminar on investing in small-cap and microcap securities shared their strategies and techniques for succeeding in this growing line of investment. Their lists of do's and don'ts provide valuable road maps for those wishing to venture beyond familiar large-cap territory.

In her opening remarks, moderator Claudia Mott notes that, in response to investor demand, small-cap funds have been steadily increasing in number in recent years. Now, microcaps are becoming increasingly popular. Definitions of these categories vary, however; different funds have different rules for inclusion. Generally, the capitalizations that are considered small range from $150 million to less than $1.5 billion; microcaps may be as large as about $500 million, according to some sources. Reflecting these loose definitions, the indexes used as performance benchmarks also vary as to which size companies they include. As the average company size has increased over the years, however, the general trend has been to raise the ceiling for inclusion in these stock categories. Mott observes also that the relationship between market size and return is generally inverse, but so is the relationship between size and risk. Return on small caps, particularly relative to large caps, appears to be cyclical, possibly because the industrial composition of the smaller companies as a group may be different from that of the larger companies and the industries themselves may have different cyclical patterns.

Although investing in microcap securities can bring large rewards, William Koenig warns that it can also bring penalties. Focused analysis of the possible hazards is essential in order to avoid shipwreck on the way to claim the treasure. In the case of microcaps, these hazards include illiquidity, unavailability of ready-made research and analysis, lack of company histories, issuance through boutiques, and the tendency for new companies to sprout and then wither on the vine from lack of support from the financial community. A second requirement for successful investment in this group of stocks, one as important as recognizing the pitfalls, is to know how to identify potential winners. The winners will be companies without inherent growth constraints, such as demand or supply limitations; companies whose success potential will be recognized by outside investors; companies that are likely to be listed soon on a major exchange; and those with talented managers. Another major aspect of success in investing in microcaps is knowing when and how to exit the investment. The ideal time is when the company has achieved the degree and type of success you had envisioned for it and is identified by the market as a winner.

Thomas Reilly and David Breed, in a joint presentation, describe their strategies for investing in small-cap firms. According to Reilly, the ideal small-cap investment is in a company that has both value and growth characteristics. Identifying such stocks early on, when they are selling at a discount, is the secret of success in small-cap investing. Above-market, although not necessarily outstanding, rates of growth are also a consideration. Reilly's firm uses both value and growth screens to narrow its list of promising small-cap stocks. From the 1,200 stocks that meet those criteria, about 100 are selected as final picks because of their quality balance sheets, generation of excess cash, reliable revenue streams, good management, and sustainable earnings growth. An essential part of the investment decision, however, is not when to buy but when to sell. The most common reasons for deciding the time to sell are a higher-than-market P/E or a market capitalization that has outgrown the firm's threshold level for small-cap stocks. The latter is the usual reason.

According to David Breed, "investing requires having one foot in the value camp and one foot in the growth camp." Four steps, in sequence, are essential to the investment process itself. The first is to generate investment ideas by finding small-cap companies that are both underpriced and have strong fundamentals and avoiding those with negative earnings surprises. A second step is to carefully research the fundamentals of those candidates selected in Step 1. What is the source of the company's earnings growth? Is that growth sustainable, or is it based on cost cutting or downsizing? Is the management accessible, and does it have the long-run interests of the company at heart? The third step is activated after a stock has been purchased. It is to monitor the firm's progress, or lack thereof: Check on the firm's revenues and feel free to ask questions about what is happening to its earnings and about changes in the market. If a stock is not performing to your expectations, figure out why. If the answer seems to be a long-term deterioration in fundamentals, then the time has come to part ways. The principal key to success in small-cap investing, as in any other type, is to maintain philosophical consistency in approach and implementation.

Daniel Ginsparg, in discussing quantitative methods for small-cap portfolio management, explains the model his firm uses to pick among the 4,000–5,000 firms in the small-company category to find those that offer the most promise. This multifactor model forecasts company fundamentals, takes into account analyst expectations about those fundamentals, and applies traditional valuation analysis to these forecasts. Several available databases are used to provide empirical information for the model, and these are checked for such problems as ticker inconsistencies, missing data, and data anomalies. Adjustments must be made for other potential problems, such as scale and calendarization. Backtesting is used to analyze company sensitivity to various factors and to study the model itself. The model can filter the data through any theoretical criteria you wish to apply. In the end, fundamental analysis is used to make the final selections. The task then becomes one of execution at reasonable cost and in reasonable time.

Research on small- and microcap stocks, says Peter Schliemann, is always a challenge. The universe not only is huge compared with large-cap companies, but it is also always changing. Companies outgrow their designations as "small" or "micro," and other fledglings come to take their places. Information on small- and microcap companies is hard to find because so few analysts cover them. The nature of the analysis also differs from that for the large-cap counterparts. The risk environment and the quality of management must be viewed differently. Like research on small companies, managing portfolios of small-cap stocks is more exacting than for larger companies. The stocks' illiquidity often has substantial price and cost effects unless traders are exceptionally patient, in which case the opportunity costs associated with waiting may also rise. Illiquidity may be a factor for clients who need to get their money out in a hurry. The number of stocks to hold in a portfolio of small-cap stocks poses a dilemma. To invest the assets of most portfolios requires holding more companies than for large-cap stocks, but a large number of companies is difficult to monitor adequately. The percentage ownership in each company is also an issue because of U.S. SEC filing requirements governing ownership of more than 5 percent of a company's stock.

Daniel Jacobs demonstrates that the small-cap effect—outperformance of small-cap stocks vis-à-vis large-cap stocks—is evident in international as well as U.S. stocks. In fact, during the past 20 years, the Europe/Australia/Far East Index, composed of large-cap international stocks, has risen by about 16 percent in contrast to the 23 percent rise for small-cap international stocks. This outperformance is pervasive throughout both developed and emerging markets, particularly on a capitalization-weighted basis. Jacobs points out that the potential amount of small-cap international stocks that will eventually become available for trading will be about $600 billion, an amount sufficient to constitute a separate asset class. A number of international small-cap indexes exist, but in most cases, their weighting tends to be skewed, according to Jacobs. Some of the new indexes that are under development will make benchmarking the performance of international small-cap stocks easier. Illiquidity is both friend and foe of international small-cap stock investors. On the one hand, it keeps these stocks relatively cheap, but on the other, it can make the cost of exiting positions very high. Jacobs' investing strategy is based on low valuation, growth (at the right price), and turnarounds. The firm looks first at the companies and then at the industry and country. Because of this bottom-up stockpicking approach, the firm's international small-cap portfolio tends to be more diversified than the indexes.

Small- and microcap stocks, because of their illiquidity, tend to be much more expensive to trade than their large-cap counterparts. John Bogle points out, however, that the size of stock is not the only variable relevant to trading cost. The size of the pool of assets under management also affects client returns. The larger amount of assets any one manager has under management, the longer the trading time involved, and the longer the trading time, the higher the transaction costs. Bogle uses a hypothetical example to show that a reduction in a manager's assets to be traded can cut trading time, and therefore costs, by a substantial amount. He emphasizes, however, that a potential conflict of interest exists in that a client's interest is in having a manager with a small asset pool whereas the manager's fee income grows as the amount of assets managed increases. Bogle suggests that performance fees could provide a resolution to this conflict by aligning the interests of client and manager. Bogle's hope is that investors begin to understand that bigger is not always better and that manager and client interests are not always the same.

The phenomenon called the "size effect" is the observable, although not necessarily consistent, outperformance of small-cap stocks compared with large-cap stocks. This relationship is evident even on a risk-adjusted basis. Marc Reinganum demonstrates that investors need not move from the largest end of the spectrum to the smallest to take advantage of the size effect—even a one-degree move can produce extra returns. He also shows that these performance differences can be very large on the upside but are not necessarily so on the downside. The size effect appears to be strongest in January, and several explanations have been proffered for this seasonality. One is tax-loss selling at the end of the year, which is reversed in January. Another is the resolution in January of information uncertainties. A third explanation is differences, by stock size, in beta; Reinganum, however, provides evidence that the market risk premiums implied by the capital asset pricing model are much greater than the actual risk premiums. Transaction cost differences between large- and small-cap stocks also are not large enough to account for the return differences. Reinganum maintains that the large-cap/small-cap differential is cyclical and predictable: Autocorrelations in five-year return differences indicate a pattern of reversals. This knowledge should help managers plan their allocations to the various size groups.

Small-Cap and Microcap Securities: An Introduction

Claudia E. Mott
Director of Small-Cap Research
Prudential Securities, Incorporated

The interest in investing in small-cap securities has grown dramatically in the past 10 years. The number of mutual funds that invest in small-cap stocks is well over 300 today, compared with fewer than 50 in 1986, and this number grows each month. Now, microcap stocks are all the rage and new funds are popping up at a number of mutual fund complexes, giving investors an opportunity to share in this part of the market.

Capitalization in the U.S. equity market is extremely concentrated—a small number of companies account for a large portion of the total. The companies in the top decile of the U.S. market account for almost 81 percent of the total market capitalization. This decile has an average market capitalization of about $7 billion. In fact, all but 2 percent of the U.S. total market capitalization is accounted for by companies with market caps greater than $125 million. In numbers of companies, however, the mass of the distribution is located in much lower capitalization levels. Hundreds of small companies have market capitalizations well below $200 million.

DEFINITIONS

What are small-cap and microcap companies? Clearly, companies that have low levels of market capitalization are small, but the question is: How small is small? Consensus is lacking on what level of capitalization constitutes a small-cap firm. Frank Russell Company, for example, considers the bottom two-thirds of the 3,000 largest U.S. companies, with capitalizations ranging from $160 million to $1 billion as the universe of small-cap firms. Wilshire Associates considers the bottom 70 percent of the largest 2,500 companies to be small-cap firms. This category includes companies with capitalizations ranging from $200 million to $1.3 billion. CRSP uses the bottom four deciles of a universe based on sorting NYSE stocks and adding stocks from Nasdaq and Amex as its definition of small cap. This definition has a few companies with extremely small capitalizations—in the $10 million range—but roughly the same upper limit as the other definition, about $1.2 billion. Standard & Poor's definition when it launched its small-cap benchmark was 600 companies between the 50th and the 83rd size percentiles of the U.S. equity market. Right now, those companies range in capitalization from about $45 million to more than $2.5 billion.

Microcap securities are a relatively new category. Although individuals have been investing in small regional companies for a long time, only recently have a large number of mutual funds paid any attention to these securities. As a result, only two satisfactory benchmarks currently exist for microcap securities: the CRSP 9–10 Index, which takes the bottom two deciles of the companies in the CRSP universe, giving this category a range from about $10 million up to about $500 million, and Callan Microcap Index, which looks at the bottom third of the largest 3,000 common stocks. Its size range, as a result, is a little bit higher than that of CRSP, as are its capitalization characteristics. Lipper Analytical Services is going to create a microcap mutual fund category sometime before the end of 1996. It is using funds that invest in stocks under $300 million. Russell also is exploring a benchmark for microcap securities created by carving the bottom 1,000 out of the Russell 2000. As with small cap, there is probably not going to be a lot of consensus on the definition of microcap.

BENCHMARK CHOICES

All these different definitions lead to differences in the capitalization characteristics of the various

---

benchmarks. Many types of indexes can be used to benchmark performance. The market value characteristics of seven of the most popular indexes used to benchmark small-cap and microcap stocks are listed in **Table 1**. For small-cap stocks, mean capitalization sizes range from $402 million for the Russell 2000 to $575 million for Wilshire's Next 1750. On the microcap side, Callan Micro has a mean capitalization of about $206 million versus the CRSP 9–10 at about $77 million. The table also shows how wide the range of companies is in those benchmarks. The median capitalizations are significantly smaller than the weighted-average amounts for each of the benchmarks.

Table 1. Market Value Characteristics: Various Equity Indexes
(billions of dollars)

Index	Weighted Average	Mean	Median
S&P 500	34.900	10.100	5.100
CRSP 9–10	0.145	0.077	0.058
Callan Micro	0.265	0.206	0.185
Russell 2000	0.527	0.402	0.334
CRSP 6–8	0.540	0.409	0.357
S&P 600	0.671	0.431	0.357
Next 1750	0.756	0.574	0.462

Source: Prudential Securities.

The most popular of these benchmarks is the Russell 2000, but the S&P small-cap index is slowly catching on because it has fewer names in it, excludes real estate investment trusts, and has a higher mean capitalization. The last characteristic is particularly attractive because the average firm size has risen a lot over time. At the upper limit, "small capitalization" now includes firms with capitalizations around $1 billion, whereas five years ago, $500 million was the upper limit on small cap. A major disadvantage of using the Russell index is that it has a very high rate of turnover—almost 25 percent of the names it contains currently (1996) will be out at the end of June 1997.

The Nasdaq was once a small-cap index, but now, its weighted-average cap is well into the billions, largely because of such companies as Microsoft Corporation and Intel Corporation, which constitute about 10 percent of the Nasdaq's total capitalization. The largest 100 companies constitute almost 40 percent of the total capitalization of the index, and the weighted-average capitalization is significantly higher than any typical small-cap fund. So, even though a lot of small-cap companies trade on the Nasdaq, the index does not really trade like a small-

cap benchmark any more and should not be considered a small-cap index.

RISK–RETURN PROFILES
The long-term cumulative performance of various asset classes is shown in **Figure 1**. As has been well documented, small-cap stocks generally outperform other asset classes. Even within equities, the smaller the stocks, the better the performance, as shown in **Figure 2**. None of this excess return, however, comes without added risk. Evident in the plot of annualized average return versus annualized standard deviation of returns shown in **Figure 3** is that the returns of smaller-cap stocks tend to be more volatile than returns from other asset classes. Although the return differential between small- and mid-cap stocks is not very large, the volatility difference is significant.

Returns from small-cap stocks also tend to run in cycles. **Figure 4** shows the relative performance of the small-cap and large-cap markets. Since 1926, small caps have outperformed large-cap stocks for a number of years in a row five times. **Table 2** details these cycles. Small-cap outperformance cycles have lasted an average of about 5.7 years, and annualized returns over these cycles have averaged about 37 percent. Small-cap stocks outperformed the S&P 500 by about 13.3 percent a year during the duration of these cycles.

A possible explanation for this cyclical behavior is sector exposures. Small-cap stocks have very different sector exposures than stocks of larger firms. The large-cap market tends to have more energy companies, consumer staples, and utilities, whereas small-cap firms are more heavily concentrated in financial services, technology, and consumer services. The performance of these industries follows cyclical patterns, and when one industry is doing well, another is usually underperforming. If utilities and energy companies are doing particularly well, the small-cap part of the market probably is not doing that well.

CONCLUSION
Although there is no consensus on the precise definition of small-cap and microcap companies, they are generally firms that are under $1 billion in capitalization. These smaller stocks have outperformed larger stocks and other asset classes during the past 70 years by about 300 basis points. This outperformance follows a cyclical pattern related to the pattern of the underlying industries that predominate among these stocks.

Table 2. Small-Cap Outperformance Cycles

Period	Duration (years)	Cumulative Return (%)	Annualized Return (%)	Excess Return versus S&P 500 (%)
1932–37	4.8	946.0	62.5	16.0
1940–45	6.0	534.1	36.0	13.9
1963–68	6.0	267.7	24.2	10.8
1975–83	8.5	1,072.6	33.6	14.5
1991–94	3.3	142.8	30.8	11.3
Average	5.7	592.6	37.4	13.3

Sources: CRSP; The University of Chicago; Prudential Securities.

Figure 1. Long-Term Performance of Various Asset Classes, 1926–95

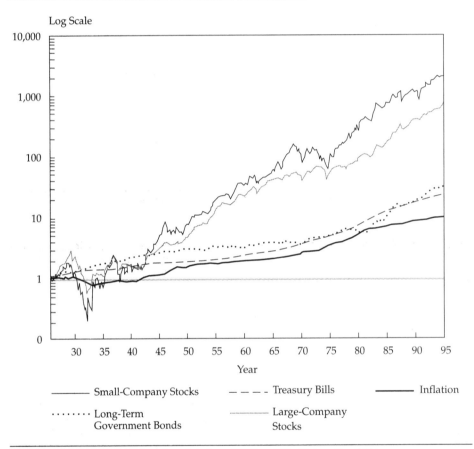

Source: Prudential Securities, based on data from CRSP and The University of Chicago.

Figure 2. Stock Performance by Market Capitalization, 1926–95

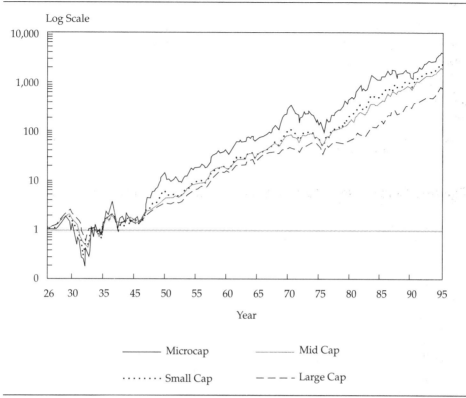

Source: Prudential Securities, based on data from CRSP and The University of Chicago.

Figure 3. Return Volatility by Market Capitalization

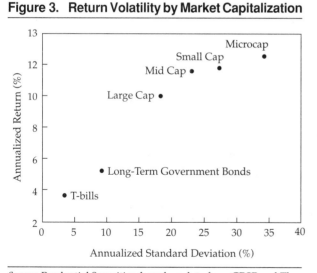

Source: Prudential Securities, based on data from CRSP and The University of Chicago.

Figure 4. Small-Cap Performance Cycles Relative to Large Cap, 1926–95

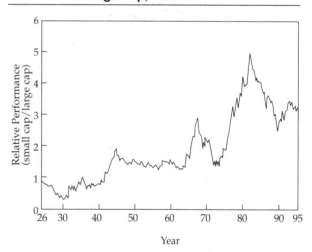

Source: Prudential Securities, based on data from CRSP and The University of Chicago.

Analysis of Microcap Securities

William D.B. Koenig, CFA
Investment Manager
Denro Fund Management Alberta Inc.

Investing in microcaps can be an adventure, with either disaster or a large payoff as an outcome. To avoid disaster, it is important to understand the limitations and hazards of these stocks before buying them. Also important is knowing when and how to exit such investments.

Microcap stocks are an exciting class of assets for investors. These very small companies, many with capitalization of less than $10 million, are the acorns that grow into oak trees. Such companies can offer a patient investor high returns, but because they have a very weak financial foundation, they can also collapse rather quickly.

CHARACTERISTICS OF THE MARKET

The microcap market is plagued by several problems. In general, microcap securities have low levels of liquidity, many become orphans (in that they receive no market coverage and have limited research and histories), and small boutiques are the lead underwriters on many financing issues.

Liquidity Concerns

Liquidity is a two-edged sword at the microcap level. Consider that if you wanted to buy 100,000 shares of IBM Corporation, you could do it at a premium of maybe 0.05 percent a share. To go into the microcap sector, with its small float, and buy 100,000 shares of any company would probably cost a 25 percent premium on any given day. This liquidity premium is critical because most investors focus on illiquidity. Too often, open-fund managers end up selling into an illiquid market, thereby hammering the market. Being in a closed-end fund resolves some of this problem because you can sell out on your own schedule. With microcaps, view the liquidity issue by not focusing on how hard the stock is to sell in weak markets but on the possible premium attainable if somebody should want to acquire this block of shares.

Limited Research

Research in microcaps is bought research. The company usually pays for outside coverage by agreeing to reserve future financial fees for the investment house supplying the research. Typically, an investment banking house that has played a role in the initial issue will provide the initial research and some coverage. Then, another house will start researching the company and, two to three months down the road, will do an equity financing for it. This sequence has happened far too many times to be purely coincidental, and often, the sudden appearance of coverage can be used to predict when a house is going to raise additional equity.

Some boutiques have good analysts, and some go through them quite often. The array of research analyst talent is extensive. We do our own analysis and rely on boutique research solely to obtain background on the companies.

Limited History

Another problem with investing in microcap securities is that many of these companies have no history. Their technologies or their adaptation of technologies are brand new, so little, if any, comparison is possible. Even when comparables are available, they typically are much larger companies that are listed on Nasdaq, so any comparisons require great care. This lack of historical data requires investors to depend to a great degree on the competence and experience of a company's management and board of directors.

Industry multiple comparisons are also not always applicable. The typical approach, at least in Canada, is to try to justify a 15 times multiple by comparing that stock with an Alberta Stock Exchange (ASE)-listed stock or by comparing, say, a high-tech stock trading at a 6–10 times multiple with a Nasdaq stock trading at a 25–40 times multiple. The reality is that the 15 times multiple price is unrealistic, so it is best to wait for the stock to come back to its proper multiple.

Small Boutiques

Boutiques are key for investing in some initial public offerings (IPOs), but a review of the history of the house that is doing the offering is important. See how well its previous offerings have done. Does it maintain adequate coverage on the stock once the offering is completed? What has it done on some of its other issues? How many of its issues have graduated to senior exchanges? Is the boutique putting out junk, or is it putting out viable companies? Is it merely a corporate fee flipper that does not care who comes through the door, or is it going to be there to help with financing the company's growth?

Orphans

We define orphans as companies that become public and very soon thereafter fizzle out from lack of exposure. No research ever appears, and the boutique that took it public abandons it. Many boutiques merely underwrite one company after another. They provide no follow-up research and are simply in the process for the investment banking fee.

The main creators of orphans are key brokers working at large houses that have huge buying power. Often, they take a small company public just on the basis of their buying power, but their follow-up research on the company is limited or nonexistent. These houses specialize in large-cap research, and doing it for small companies is not profitable. So, the stock performance of what could otherwise be a good company could remain poor because nobody knows the company exists. Unless the broker has the capability of generating interest among the boutiques, this stock is stymied.

WHAT TO LOOK FOR

Clearly, a microcap security must offer unlimited potential; otherwise, it will forever remain an acorn. A company may have nothing hindering its current success, but we look forward to how that company could grow to the next stage and what would happen to it if it did. This approach requires knowing each company's key success-recognition factors. We also look for companies that have blue-chip capability, that is, the ability to move to a senior exchange. The final and most important attribute of a potential winner is the presence of a solid management team.

Unlimited Upside

One of the attributes we look for in a company is the absence of preimposed limitations. Many of these companies have good initial growth, but their future growth is constrained by such external factors as technology, regulation, demand, and limited markets for their products. Many companies that license technology for a particular geographical area end up with an upper cap on their growth. As an example, a company may want to put up a hotel complex in

Banff (Alberta), an area with lots of hotels. The problem is that only so many people can stay in those rooms, and at some point in time, the company's growth will flatten out.

Identifying the problem of limited upside in a company requires careful and painstaking analysis. An analyst cannot rely solely on the company's management to provide the right story. Often, a stock gets hyped both by management and by other outside investors, but an analyst should be very skeptical of such signals. Consider the downside risk, and analyze what would happen if the company failed. We do not invest in a company if use of our proceeds would erase more than 25 percent of the stock value. Dreaming of potential rewards if the company actually takes off is easy, but with microcap securities, examining downside risk is critical. The key question is whether the cost of failure would be greater than the reward for success.

Success Recognition

A success-recognition factor is one in which the market rewards stocks with higher multiples based on the company's initial success. For example, an exploration company set out to look for diamonds in Labrador and came up with one of the biggest nickel finds in the world. Recently, the company was sold for C$40 billion, although it had never mined an ounce of nickel. The key was that the market was prepared to give it the full value of the find merely for drilling certain core samples and defining the area. A similar phenomenon occurs in oil and gas, another resource play. For locking up the land, drilling an initial well, and discovering a new pool, the market will typically reward the company for a good percentage of the value of the pool.

When making such investments, knowing the success-recognition factors in advance and the timing of the various success events is useful. Stocks of mining and oil-drilling companies are fairly simple in this regard. They have a time line; investors know when they are going to get results. Biotechnology stocks are slightly different. The process has three stages: clinical trials, Food and Drug Administration (FDA) approval, and production. Because a government agency is involved, the final production time is less predictable than for other endeavors. Many small biotechnology companies do not have the financial support to wait months for FDA approval, and that is why we tend to avoid those firms. Too often, we see investors selling the stock before the proceeds have even been spent.

Blue-Chip Capability

Blue-chip capability implies that a company can move fairly fast and fairly quickly to a listing on a senior exchange. Typically, the companies we invest in come out on the ASE and move fairly rapidly to the Toronto Stock Exchange (TSE) or Nasdaq. This listing on a larger exchange provides higher stock multiples and, importantly, the liquidity for our exit strategies. Oil and gas stocks, for example, will trade on the smaller exchanges at 3 to 4 times cash flow, but when they get on the TSE, the multiples increase to 5 or 6. On Nasdaq, the multiple may be 8 to 10.

Having a listing on a major exchange also attracts greater research coverage. A lot of funds will not look at companies listed on small regional exchanges, but as soon as the stocks get to the senior boards, they become worthy of coverage. The movement up to a senior exchange also provides a company with access to lower cost capital and lower dilution as the stock's price level increases. The key to this strategy is to look for companies that are likely to move to a senior board fairly quickly.

Management

Good management is critical for a microcap company's success. These companies depend heavily upon management and its capabilities, and for many, success depends on only one or two key individuals. Investment managers must be actively involved in getting rid of nonperformers. Having influence, in our case, usually involves taking a board seat or an officer position in the company. Small companies cannot afford to have an officer on rehabilitation or whatever for any length of time. If people are not performing, they should be replaced fairly quickly. Surprisingly, the officer that we have most often replaced is the chief financial officer.

Avoid managers who treat their work as a job. Do not hire people who want to come in at 8:00 and leave at 4:30, have four weeks of holiday, and are more concerned about getting a fifth week than getting the project done. You want people who have their lives on the line. Their jobs are their sweat and blood.

The character of the board members is also important. In the United States, board members generally serve a purpose, and that is beginning to be the case in Canada. With microcaps, many board members are just friends of the person who came to the board with the most money. We also prefer to stay away from companies in which board members are known stock promoters.

WHAT TO AVOID

Investors should avoid several things when investing in microcap securities. The most obvious is overpopulated sectors, but other factors to consider include copycats of popular themes and low earnings growth.

Overpopulated Sectors

At the moment, Internet stocks are probably the most overpopulated. People come out with the latest software and seek backing in a field that is still plagued with questionable commercial value. New companies with new claims and new products start up every day. You never know when you will have a hit and when you will not, but in general, in the absence of some compelling reason, try to stay away from those sectors.

Promoter Themes

A popular business strategy is to imitate a company soon after its idea or product takes off. The imitators follow a popular theme, and they get investors to buy in. The stock of an Alberta company that discovered gold in Indonesia went from C$2.00 to C$200.00. Within three months of this company's breaking into the market and becoming a high-rising stock, 20 other companies suddenly had gold claims in Indonesia. Be very careful with these types of deals because most do not work. You might be better off investing in the original company.

Steady Growth

A company may offer assured and steady growth at 15 percent a year, but why would you want to go for 15 percent growth, especially if, for the same level of risk, you could get 100 percent growth? In the microcap market, with its high level of risk, the idea is to "go big or go home." Throw the dice, because that is where the biggest rewards lie.

EXIT STRATEGIES

The timing of the exit strategy is as important in microcap securities as is finding the right company. Clearly, achieving the success-recognition factor is important because that is an indication that the time has come to exit.

A typical exit strategy is to let company presidents know of your intention to sell. Typically, they will know of buyers wanting to buy blocks of stock. You should have some concern about exiting until the company moves to a senior exchange and starts receiving appropriate multiples. Let the stock make its move, let it get noticed, before exiting.

SUCCESSFUL PICKS AND WHY

Some of our more successful picks are described in **Table 1**. One was a small exploration company, Baytex Energy Ltd., whose stock had come out at 40 cents and within a year had moved to more than C$3.00. The company's production grew from 100 barrels of oil a day in 1993 to a projected average of more than 7,000 barrels a day for 1997. The president is a proven, aggressive, talented explorationist. He had very good initial success. In this instance, the stock moved on to the senior exchange, and it is now

Table 1. Six Successful Picks

Company	Product	Purchase Price (C$)	Characteristics
Baytex Energy	Oil and gas	3.00	Managers were proven explorationists; pedigree of its search area was good; initial success moved the stock from $0.40 to $3.00 in less than a year
Ceramics Protection	Bulletproof vests and related products	2.00	High-growth industry of the future; key board figures; profitable existing business, with proprietary technology and strong niche opportunities
Pelorus Navigation	Global positioning system-based aeronautics instrumentation	2.00	Key agreement with Honeywell to market its main product; significant jump on competitors; strong boutique doing the placement
B&W Technologies (private company)	Gas-detection monitoring equipment	na	Marketing efforts undercapitalized; technology lead over competitors; modernization of product line; production costs decreasing; sales increasing
Interaction Resources	Oil and gas	0.40	Strong explorationist team; pedigree of search area strong; currently working on home-run play that could add $1.40 per share value or $0.25 decrease for failure
VICOM Multimedia	Multimedia production and software	1.00	Core existing business with solid management; completing three new software products for the publishing sector

na = not applicable.

Source: Denro Fund Management.

being given a multiple of 6 for its 1997 cash flow. We believed it was a good time to exit, and the stock is now trading at about C$14.00.

Another example of a successful recent pick is Ceramics Protection Corporation, a company that makes bulletproof vests using ceramics and Kevlar. We saw in this company a proprietary technology and strong niche opportunities in a high-growth industry and the presence of some key board members who had the "right stuff." The proceeds were used to expand from one to three kilns. The company is currently testing the new kilns. When sales begin, I suspect that the stock will start moving up rapidly as sales increase.

Pelorus Navigation Systems is a company with a two-stage success factor. The first stage was a deal with Honeywell that gave the company's product a lot of credibility. Honeywell has about 80 percent of the avionics market, and the agreement is that Honeywell will market Pelorus's product, a new type of landing system for aircraft. The second stage, which is still pending, is a review by the U.S. Federal Aviation and Aeronautics (FAA) Board that could make this system its product of choice for airports. In this instance, because we have been in the stock such a short time, we will wait for FAA approval before exiting.

B&W Technologies Ltd. is a company that makes gas-detection monitoring equipment for industrial and personal use. It makes a small clip-on device that detects the presence of dangerous gases.

The company was engineering rich but marketing poor—nothing that money could not solve. It subsequently hired one of the industry's top-rated salesmen to be its vice president of sales. He is now building up the distribution network, and the company's sales have ramped up accordingly. We are in the process of taking this company public.

Interaction Resources is an oil and gas company. The success factor we are waiting for is the announcement of results from the company's exploration tests. Conservatively, the estimate is that favorable results will add almost $1.40 per share in value, and we will be rewarded handsomely. Even if the results are not favorable, the company still has a strong exploration team and good search areas.

VICOM Multimedia is an 18-year-old multimedia company. It got into the production of training software and software for analyzing circuit boards. When it was building the product, it came up with a revolutionary way of handling multimedia files that led to a whole new publishing system. The company went to the market in April or May and raised C$10 million at C$2.25; the company still has C$9 million of this secondary offering. The stock has since been as low as C$1.30 and now sits at about C$1.50. This company will do six trade shows by November 1996. How the market receives the products will tell us whether we want to exit or hang on. Our success factor is how this product is going to do at the trade shows.

Question and Answer Session

William D.B. Koenig, CFA

Question: Please discuss some of your unsuccessful investments and why they did not work.

Koenig: With the majority of companies, we are waiting for the success factors to occur. To date, we have had two recognized failures. One was a company on which the only one that made any money was the underwriter. Each time that boutique was involved, the company lost more and more value. We no longer do business with that boutique. The second failure was a technology company. It had a great idea, but it did not get the product to the market.

When we invest at this level, we have the advantage of still having a public shell and tax pools if the company fails, and we will roll those assets into another company that has a good idea and catch a ride on its coattails. By using this strategy, we have a chance of recouping some of our initial investment. We have divested the first company and are currently cleaning up the second for resale.

Question: Do you use any particular indexes to compare your performance against?

Koenig: No, because of the investment constraints we have. We are not a normal fund compared with others. We can only invest in Treasury issues when the proceeds are spent in Alberta. Also, we are not looking at the outcome as a rate of return. We are looking for when the success factors will occur, which will tell us what our valuation is. We are patient enough to say that if it takes two years for the factor to occur, then we will wait for two years and

see what we get. As a fund, we are only two years old, so we are quite new at this type of investing.

Question: How do you evaluate management stock options? Is there a point at which management has too much in the way of stock options?

Koenig: Everybody hates to have the managers suddenly take some profit on a stock option, because they do not know how to read that move. Yet, stock options are an integral part of managers' compensation. For what the managers of these new companies go through, their salary is not great, so you have to reward them on the stock side. In Canada, stock options are limited to 10 percent of the value of the shares outstanding, which is a reasonable number.

Question: Have you found good names among orphans? Are there companies that can easily be turned around?

Koenig: The problem we have with orphans is that unless they are doing a new issue, because of the investing rules of our fund, we cannot get involved with them. If I were to run a fund that is totally separate and I were the only investor, I know of several good orphans that would be great companies. The ASE has more than 800 companies listed on it. The bulk of them would be microcaps.

Question: What is the fund's two-year rate of return?

Koenig: We have not actually calculated it. Again, we are not looking at rate of return. Out of the 20 equity investments we have

made, the value of two companies is up more than 300 percent. We have about six companies that have increased between 100 and 200 percent, but for some others, we are still waiting for their success factors to occur. We have about 13 companies on which we are either up as much as 100 percent or down about 50 percent. Again, their success factors have not occurred. Right now, the result is too early to call. Within another year, we could probably start putting out a half-decent rate of return number, but the criterion is different from most investments. A lot of these companies do not even have a history or have yet to fully spend the money we have invested in them.

Question: With 800 companies on the ASE, do you use some method or set of tools to screen through that universe looking for quality small-cap and microcap companies?

Koenig: No, because I am limited to secondary offerings or IPOs. Our preference has been to go with IPOs, so quantitative analysis does not come into play.

Question: Have you found a difference in the performance of IPO companies and those you have purchased as seasoned equity?

Koenig: Yes, in the sense that some of these companies will come out and have a lot of shares outstanding. You will not get quite the return that you would if you helped structure the deal from the start. If the number of shares is limited, your earnings, or your cash flow multiple, are much better. The biggest problem we find is that a lot of companies have junked themselves up with too many shares at too small a price initially. You cannot blame the companies. At this level, they are desperate for cash, so they will do whatever it takes to carry on with the project. In some cases, they do not have any foresight about the effect of issuing too many shares in the future. Their attitude is let's get it done and move on.

Question: How long are you willing to wait for operating cash for a development-stage company?

Koenig: We very rarely invest at the development stage. Typically, we like a company with a core business to which it is adding a product. A perfect example is VICOM Multimedia. It had been a profitable multimedia business for 18 years when it decided to get into publishing software. It had a core business that it could rely on to carry the earnings. The new products, if successful, would add value.

Question: What are the requirements for getting on the ASE compared with some of the other stock exchanges in Canada?

Koenig: The main requirement that is unique to the ASE is the junior capital pool, which is a blind pool. Investors will invest up to half a million dollars in a shell company, and then the company has to do a major transaction. Many private companies use this procedure to go public. Also, in Canada, each province is responsible for its governance of the exchange. Oversight in Vancouver has been lax, and although the rumor is that the government is trying to tighten it up, we have not been convinced. To date, we have done only one deal on the Vancouver Stock Exchange. All of the rest have been on the ASE because, in our opinion, it maintains tighter rules and regulations.

Question: How do you value companies that hit initial success factors but their momentum eventually decreases?

Koenig: Baytex is a perfect example of this. That company has had huge growth in oil production but is unlikely to be able to maintain it. The growth rate will likely slow down to about 30 percent from the current pace of 200–300 percent, a signal for us to exit and put our cash in faster growing companies. Again, the strategy depends on your level of risk preference. I am paid to be a pony player and to make big bets.

Question: Do you invest only in private placements or in registered shares, and if so, how are you valuing private placements?

Koenig: We have done two private companies. We typically invest in a combination of straight equity and convertible debentures. We let the company know up front that we have use of our proceeds in this fund for five years, that we will work out an exit strategy, and that it will likely be to take the company public. The ASE serves as a very good vehicle for that, and if the company is at all successful with its endeavors, we take it to the market fairly fast. Also, we would be considered insiders of the company when it is private, and we would probably be escrowed for three years. That is one of the reasons we want to take companies public as fast as possible, to get the escrow provisions cleared up.

Strategies for Investing in Small-Cap Firms: Part I

Thomas V. Reilly, CFA
Managing Director
Putnam Investment Management

Much has been written about the relative advantages of growth and value investing. Investing in small-cap stocks with above-average earnings growth and low P/Es delivers top-performing returns at relatively low levels of volatility. The strategy also encourages low turnover, adding to the net return advantage of such an investor.

Money managers can emphasize many types of stocks—large-cap growth, small-cap growth, large-cap value, small-cap value, and so forth. Although value investing is quite different from growth investing, our experience has shown that investing in small-cap stocks with above-average growth and strong value characteristics produces high sustainable performance with relatively low risk.

The universe of small-cap companies is very large. More than 4,600 listed companies have market capitalizations between $50 million and $1 billion. The challenge is to narrow this universe to a small usable sample of firms with the relevant characteristics.

SMALL-CAP VALUE INVESTMENT PHILOSOPHY

Our investment philosophy on the small-cap side can be best described as investing in companies with above-average growth that sell at a discount. The typical small-cap manager has a higher hurdle rate for growth than one investing in large-cap firms. Minimum growth rates of 17–20 percent a year are not unusual for small-cap firms. Small-cap value managers also look for above-average growth but at rates well below that of the minimum hurdle rate of most small-cap growth managers. Over time, this more moderate but still above-average rate of growth is much more sustainable than a higher rate. By investing in these above-average growth companies that sell at a discount to the market, we are able to achieve returns of the best small-cap managers but at much lower levels of volatility.

Only a small percentage of the potential investments in the small-cap sector, about 400 companies, grow at a rate in the 17–20 percent range. High-growth companies have extremely high betas and P/Es and often experience severe liquidity constraints.

The small-cap growth universe is also very concentrated: Almost all of the 200 managers who call themselves small-cap growth managers own the same 400 stocks. The companies are typically in the anointed industries of today, which include technology, health care, and telecommunications. Despite the claim of most growth managers that they are looking at the long term, their interests tend to focus on the industries that are currently popular.

The result of this stampede into (and out of) popular sector bets is often high levels of volatility. These are stocks of fairly small companies, and if hundreds of managers try to buy the same small stocks at the same time, the stocks go up dramatically and quickly become very expensive. Similarly, when the momentum of the 20 percent growth rate disappears, all the growth managers try to get out at the same time, resulting in a sudden, sharp decline in stock prices.

SMALL-CAP VALUE/GROWTH

Since 1987, when our firm started investing in small-cap stocks, our focus has been on stocks that other small-cap growth managers ignore. Our process consists of a screen that identifies value companies—those having P/Es lower than the market P/E—and also those companies with above-average growth rates. Historically, the average rate of earnings growth among S&P 500 Index companies has been about 6 percent a year; so, above-average growth does not have to mean 20 percent. Stocks of companies with earnings growth rates of 8–15 percent are acceptable as long as those rates are sustainable.

Our belief is that these firms will not sell at a discount forever and that by buying them cheap, we can take advantage of the revaluation when it occurs. This style requires patience, however. Revaluation that occurs through the trading process is slow, especially among small-cap stocks because so little investment firepower is trained on these stocks.

Our investment strategy also concentrates on dividend-paying stocks. Our screening process provides about 1,200 companies from the small-cap universe. Of these, about 700 pay dividends. Many dividend-paying small-cap stocks sell at a discount to the market and provide a yield advantage that can give a money manager a leg up on the Russell 2000 Index or on other small-cap growth managers. Most of these companies have above-average growth rates, low P/Es, and low betas.

Interest in small-cap value stocks is limited to a few managers, and such stocks receive little Wall Street coverage—on average, five or six analysts per stock. In contrast, Wall Street scrutiny of small-cap growth firms is fairly intense, averaging about 19 analysts covering each firm. One of the advantages of investing in small-cap value stocks is that the herd is concentrated in the high-growth stocks. The faster the growth rate, the more analysts follow the stock and the higher the P/E. Small-cap growth stocks are fairly efficiently priced and hence offer fewer bargains.

The small-cap stocks that pass through both the growth and the value screens are not actively covered and have small institutional ownership (42 percent compared with 73 percent for growth stocks). Hence, they provide a substantial opportunity.

THE BUY DECISION

Our eventual investment decision, the buy decision, is the culmination of our screening process. We narrow the universe of small-cap stocks by first picking those that meet our guidelines: above-average growth rates, strong value characteristics, and sparse Wall Street following. From the remaining sample, about 1,200 stocks, we identify those companies with quality balance sheets, excess cash generation, recurring revenue streams, good management, and (above all) sustainable earnings growth. The end result is about 100 stocks diversified among interest-sensitive sectors (10–20 percent), industrials (40–45 percent), and consumer goods (40–45 percent).

The key to our strategy is to find the best value among companies that are likely to be around for a long time. We want to be able to invest for the long term. This focus on the long term has allowed us to keep our annual stock turnover down to 33 percent of the stocks in the portfolio. In contrast, many growth managers switch all the stocks in their portfolios in any given year. Our low turnover rate helps to contain transaction costs, thus allowing us to outperform the market, net of transaction costs, despite relatively modest returns.

THE SELL DECISION

To lock in profits from our investment strategy, we have developed a strong sell discipline. Our equity team sells a stock when the P/E gets higher than that of the market (the S&P 500). Not every stock in the portfolio has a lower-than-market P/E, but certainly more than 90 percent of the stocks do. The others generally remain in the portfolio for a very short period of time. If the P/Es get measurably above that of the market, the stocks have to go.

Another reason for selling the stock is if the market cap gets above a certain level. We periodically adjust this threshold upward, generally to keep up with market movements—currently, the ceiling is $1.5 billion, up from $1.25 billion. We want to take advantage of the diversification benefits associated with small-cap firms; when the firms get too large—say, more than $2 billion in market cap—they start acting like their large-cap brethren.

Other reasons for putting a stock on the sell list is if the company's fundamentals deteriorate substantially and our in-house research shows that sustainable earnings growth is no longer possible. In addition, if a stock's valuation gets unattractive compared with peer stocks, we sell that stock. For example, if we have a bank stock with a P/E of 12, but every other bank stock with above-average growth is selling at 10 times earnings, we attempt to sell our bank stock and put that money into cheaper stocks.

Our experience has been that 80 percent of the total stock turnover comes from the first two constraints: P/E and market cap. In other words, the turnover comes about in a good way. Instead of having to get out of a stock because of a slow-down in momentum, as most growth managers do, we get out because the stocks get too big or too expensive. Those reasons are a lot more acceptable than trying to justify why a firm may have not met its earnings estimate for a quarter. We are not looking for 20 percent growth. A growth rate of 10 percent a year does not frighten us, even though the company had a down quarter, if the company is expected to continue to grow at about 10 percent thereafter. If we think we have to pay too much for this 10 percent grower, however, we do want to get out.

PORTFOLIO CHARACTERISTICS

We run two small-cap portfolios, one that invests in dividend-paying stocks (Small-Cap Value I) and one in which dividends are optional (Small-Cap Value II). **Table 1** shows the characteristics of these two portfolios.

Most small-cap growth portfolios today have much higher median capitalizations than ours do, because they have a tough time finding small stocks to substitute for those that become too big. As a result, many of these "overgrown" stocks get left in the portfolio, which balloons its median capitalization.

The financial characteristics of the companies we invest in show that, although we are clearly value investors, we do not sacrifice quality to get value. As long as investors are willing to look beyond the three, four, or five market-anointed industries, they can find companies with above-average growth rates. You have to be willing to live with companies that may not be that exciting—lawn mower companies and companies that supply bearings, for example.

For our Value II portfolio, turnover is only about a third of the companies in the portfolio, which translates to about 70 percent in dollar turnover. The discrepancy between number and dollar turnover occurs because we typically buy when a stock moves down and sell when it is moving up. Thus, during the year, we can trim our portfolios by selling into strength and buying into weakness.

CONCLUSION

Putnam's small-cap value/growth strategy consists of investing in firms with above-average growth, low P/Es, and strong fundamentals. By not chasing the firms with extremely high earnings growth, this strategy delivers substantial sustainable returns at low levels of volatility. Although growth investing will be superior during some periods, the performance of our value/growth strategy relative to the S&P 500 and the Russell 2000, on both returns and risk, shows us that our strategy is clearly a dominant one.

Table 1. Portfolio Characteristics: Small-Cap Value Equities, as of June 30, 1996

Characteristic	Putnam Small-Cap Value II	Putnam Small-Cap Value I	Russell 2000
Capitalization			
Median	$251 million	$509 million	$340 million
Weighted average	350 million	522 million	410 million
Financial attributes			
P/E	14.3×[a]	13.5×[a]	18.4×[b]
Dividend yield	0.5%	2.6%	1.5%
Return on equity	18.1[a]	15.6[a]	12.1
Debt/capital	26.9	23.7	37.0
Earnings growth (next five years)	15.2	10.9	NA[c]
Portfolio description			
Annual turnover	70%		
Cash position	0–10%		
Number of holdings	125[a]		

[a]Based on 1996 estimates.
[b]Based on trailing 12 months, excluding negative earnings.
[c]Not available for five-year projection.

Source: Putnam Investment Management.

Strategies for Investing in Small-Cap Firms: Part II

David B. Breed, CFA
Managing Director and Chief Investment Officer
Cadence Capital Management

Value and growth considerations should both be part of a comprehensive investment strategy. Stock picking should be an orderly process consisting of several steps and aimed at identifying promising stocks and rejecting those with negative attributes.

The debate about the virtues of investing in growth versus value stocks is ongoing. Proponents of growth stocks argue that investing in firms with high earnings growth is more likely to result in sustained profits than bottom fishing for low-priced stocks. Cheap stocks, the growth investors contend, deserve to be cheap because they represent companies that have very poor potential. Proponents of value investing rely on empirical evidence that stocks of low-P/E firms outperform stocks of high-P/E firms. They argue that what you pay for the stock now is a more important determinant of total return than the company's expected growth.

A well-developed investment strategy is a combination of growth and value approaches. The conundrum that faces us as investors is: Why do stocks go up? They go up because the dynamics of the underlying company change. At the same time, although we are looking for companies with good earnings dynamics, we want to make sure that everybody else has not already figured out the true value. So, in essence, investing requires having one foot in the value camp and one foot in the growth camp.

THE INVESTMENT PROCESS

A good investment process should identify good potential investment opportunities. The process is much like the assembly line used in building a car. It has several phases:

- the generation of investment ideas,
- qualitative research,
- purchase and follow-up research, and
- the sell decision.

Generating Investment Ideas

The generation of investment ideas is a very im-portant step in the assembly line because it permits analysts to narrow the list of potential companies to a manageable subset.

Excluding the top 1,000 market-capitalization issues from the universe of companies leaves about 3,000 small-cap companies as potential candidates. Doing fundamental research on all of these companies is a long, arduous process that involves a lot of time and has no clear benefits.

You must have some place to start. You could wait for sell-side analysts to call you, but the first call will go to some big mutual fund that has huge amounts to invest, not to you. You might start by looking at companies with improving fundamentals. Who are these companies, and how do you find out about them? Again, you could wait for the call, but you are not likely to get a call on companies that are clear winners with excellent fundamentals.

You could look for stocks that are relatively cheap, which sounds easy. You could look for stocks that have a high dividend yield or low price-to-book or price-to-earnings ratios, but the problem with starting there is distinguishing between a cheap stock and a lousy company. Lots of bad companies are cheap because they deserve to be cheap.

What is required is to find companies that are both underpriced *and* have strong fundamentals. A good investment process should look for stocks with improving fundamentals and valuations that are reasonable. A sound screening process that generates potential investment candidates with good attributes is more likely to catch something worthwhile than simply throwing the line out randomly.

What are good attributes to look for in stocks? The best reasons to own stock are

- rapid expected earnings per share (EPS) growth,

- accelerating earnings momentum,
- high and rising return on equity (ROE),
- high and rising cash flow return on investment, and
- rising earnings estimates.

Companies with rapid expected EPS growth are the acorns that grow into oak trees. Finding such acorns is why investing in small-cap stocks is so attractive. Other good factors would be accelerating earnings momentum and a high and rising ROE financed by high and rising return on investment for companies for which analysts' estimates of earnings are going up. If you can find all five of those characteristics, you clearly have a winning investment, but only one or two of the five is often enough.

At the same time, companies with negative attributes should be avoided. These characteristics include

- negative earnings surprises,
- high price-to-earnings ratio,
- high price-to-book ratio,
- high price-to-cash-flow ratio, and
- high price-to-revenues ratio.

The first and foremost attribute to avoid is negative earnings surprises, because a negative surprise announcement always adversely affects a portfolio. Also, disappointing earnings tend to go on for five to six quarters in a row as management scurries around trying to fix the unfixable.

Other factors to avoid are at the opposite end of the value spectrum—for example, paying too high a price for the stock. Investing in high-P/E stocks is not a profitable strategy. Every credible study shows that over any meaningful time frame, investing in low-P/E stocks, low price-to-book stocks, and high-yield stocks works. It works because avoiding extremely high valuations works. Stay away from what we like to call a "high price-to-concept ratio"—a company with a market capitalization of $2 billion that has never been profitable. These investments might work for a month or two, but then they crash and burn.

Qualitative Research

Once you have identified good candidates, you should focus on the qualitative research needed to understand the company's underlying fundamentals.

To identify firms with high profit growth, try to understand what is driving those profits. A company's sources of profit growth and the sustainability of those sources are clearly an important part of the qualitative research required in the investment process. The DuPont formula is a good way to break down a company's profitability into three sources: rising revenues, improving margins, and changes in leverage.

It is important to understand whether the company's earnings growth is coming from revenue increases because of, say, new products and new markets or shifts into more profitable product mixes. Or, is it coming from less desirable and less sustainable sources, such as product price increases? Revenue growth that is driven by higher product prices is not sustainable.

Cost cutting through massive employee layoffs has recently been a major theme with large-cap firms. But this form of profit growth is not sustainable. After all, how many more employees can be cut by a company that just laid off 25,000 workers? Fortunately, this layoff phenomenon has not yet caught on with the small-cap firms. For them, earnings growth is still determined in large part by revenue growth.

Another factor to look for is a company's ability to make accretive acquisitions. One of the major themes in industry today is consolidation. Smaller companies are growing by making synergistic acquisitions of other, even smaller operations.

In addition to explaining the sources of profit growth, good qualitative research should unearth the underlying motives for managerial decisions. At this end of the marketplace, analyst coverage is very poor. You have to rely on your own resources and your own intuition to follow what is going on with company management.

One of the pleasant aspects of small- and micro-cap stocks is that when you telephone the company, you do not talk to the assistant vice president in charge of investor relations but with the person in charge or the person sitting next to the person in charge. This direct contact assures that the information is timely.

Be careful of the growth-at-any-price company manager who insists on building unit volume by cutting prices. This kind of approach leads to profitless prosperity and should be avoided. In the generic drug industry, for example, every time a new drug comes off patent, a number of companies start making the drug and selling it at very low margins, with the result that none of them makes any profit.

Also avoid managers who are expensive caretakers who took over from the founder. Is the company being run by people who are committed to the company's success, or is it just a playground for the next generation?

Some managers merely want to fix their companies' problems and sell them off. Such companies are not necessarily growth companies that are going to continue for the next 50 years, but they can be very good stocks. When the final objective is the company's sale, the managers may engage in serious cost cutting, because they probably own the stock.

Finally, examine whether management's motives are tied up with those of the stockholders. Do the managers own the stock, and what percentage of their compensation is tied to stock performance?

Follow-Up Research

The investment process does not end with identifying and purchasing a set of companies with good products in good markets and good management that looks out for the interests of the shareholders. The stocks must be monitored continuously to ensure that they are not an anchor on the portfolio. What is going on with revenues, products that were supposed to generate those revenues, the markets the company was supposed to penetrate, and profit margins from products are all issues that need to be monitored.

Be a skeptic! Once you own a company's stock, you have every right to call up and inquire why a company's actual earnings were lower than its estimated earnings. Is the company still gaining market share? Are competitive pressures entering the market? Is product transition going as fast as it should? Management might provide every explanation and promise that its statistics will be better next year, but remember that the long run is merely a series of short runs stuck together, so the short run does count. Make sure that what you think is going to happen is what is actually happening; if it is not, then it is time to go on to the next stock.

Sell Decisions

If a stock is not working out, take a hard look at why it is not performing. If the trends in revenues and margins do not meet expectations, reconsider holding the stock. The company might still be doing well—20 percent growth sounds great unless you were expecting 40 percent—but is this lower-than-expected performance the result of an unusual event or is it symptomatic of a long-term decline in company fundamentals? Shipping an order in October when it should have been shipped in September or writing off an underperforming asset in the hope of improving the business mix down the road are examples of events from which recovery is easy. For an insurance company, however, to claim large insurance losses on property damage resulting from a hurricane is not a recoverable event, because that is the business the insurance company is in—anticipating and making contingencies for such events. Be a skeptic and do not be afraid to sell a company if you are not convinced that its problems are short term and easily reversible.

THE KEY TO SUCCESS

Whether you are managing money or finding managers to manage money for you, the key to finding good small-cap stocks with strong fundamentals is a *philosophically consistent* investment approach. Without this consistency, analysts may be taking different approaches or portfolio managers may not even talk to the analysts. With philosophically consistent implementation across portfolios, everybody is in sync, attention is focused on the same end, and all extraneous matters are avoided. Consistency is the most important part of this business. Distractions, such as incessant telephone calls or a ton of paper coming across the desk, can take away from the primary mission. Much of this inconsistency is the result of not knowing what types of stocks you would like to consider for the portfolio. Conviction gets you through periods when nothing seems to work.

CONCLUSION

Make sure that your investment process is implemented consistently. Ultimately, growth works, and in the long run, value works, but if you keep swapping back and forth from one to the other, you are very likely to be in the wrong portfolio at the wrong time.

Question and Answer Session

David B. Breed, CFA
Thomas V. Reilly, CFA

Question: The number of stocks in the small-cap universe is fairly large—about 4,600, according to Thomas Reilly's presentation. Are you using computerized databases and screening services to narrow the list? Which are you using? How are you using them?

Breed: Yes, we do use outside database services, and we combine a lot of different ones. We use both Zachs Investment Research and First Call Corporation for earnings estimates. We also use Bloomberg and other financial data and trading systems. First Call is a very good service for keeping up with earnings estimates and so forth. As a firm, we probably actively use 60 different brokerage firms; 10 are Wall Street research firms, and 50 are not. Some of the 50 are pure trading firms that do not have research, but the bulk of them are regional brokerage houses that either are not on First Call or do not have estimates plugged into some of those sources. With small-cap stocks, the regional brokers are the people to talk with. So, although having the databases is helpful for building the fish finder, they are not sufficient. You still have to do the work and get on the phone. Being proactive is better than being reactive.

Reilly: The small-cap value universe changes very slowly. When we started our small-cap value product at the end of 1987, I asked our computer people to look for lower-than-market P/Es, market caps between $50 million and $1 billion, histories of above-average growth, and paid dividends. That gave us 700 stocks. As I looked at the list of the 700 stocks, I saw mostly the same names that I had seen in 1980, when I started this product at another firm.

Block Drug Company, for example, a company headquartered in Jersey City, New Jersey, has had about one down year since it went public in 1973, so it meets the growth criteria. It has certainly had double-digit earnings—not 15 percent, but 10–12 percent. It did get expensive twice in the past 20 years: when the company first offered the stock in 1973 and all drug stocks were in favor and in 1991, when again, all drug stocks were in favor. That is how some of these small-cap value stocks are revalued upward enough so that they do not meet our criteria any more: They are in an industry that Wall Street anoints as a growth industry.

Typically, our computer screens show the same names over and over again, which makes the job simpler because you are calling the same companies over and over again. It also makes the process much more sustainable. You do not have to figure out which companies to look at next, because they are the same ones you were looking at before.

Question: Please talk about the optimum number of holdings for assets under management. How many stocks do you own, and has that number changed over time?

Reilly: When we started out, we had a small amount of money and a small number of names, but that situation has changed. We built this product to be a vehicle for managing significant money. Our Small-Cap I portfolio averages about 140 stocks. Our Small-Cap II portfolio averages about 130 stocks. Perhaps 10 or 15 names overlap the two portfolios, but most of the names in I are not in II, so between the two, we own 250 stocks of the 1,200 stocks that meet our initial criteria. The 700-company universe that we ran in 1987 beat the market. In other words, once we set up the criteria, we are fishing in a pond that gives us a leg up on the market. We ask each of our portfolio managers to compete against a normal portfolio, and our portfolio managers have beaten the norm, although not by huge amounts, but the norm has significantly beaten the Russell 2000 index.

Breed: I am not sure what the precise optimal number of holdings would be, but since its inception in 1988, our firm has had 80–100 stocks in our small-cap portfolios. We believe the characteristics of the portfolio count more than any one name. To have performance that is ultimately sustainable and believable by our clientele, we do not want it to depend upon one or two home runs; it should depend upon a good batting average.

As for dollars of assets under management, we closed our small-cap product at $250 million. It is at $800 million today, and we are not adding any net assets to that. Our definition of "small cap" is fairly typical. It includes firms in the $100 million to $1 billion range. By our definition, firms that are smaller than $100 million are classified as microcap.

Question: What benchmarks do your companies use for the small-cap value portfolios?

Breed: We began in 1988 as a small-cap core manager. The growth versus value debate has since become popular, but we have not changed our spots in response. The universe we use for virtually all of our clients is the Russell 2000, which is reported in the newspaper every day. It is publicly available and generally accepted. Other indexes are acceptable, but the Russell seems to be the one that everybody likes. Although the S&P 500 Index is not necessarily relevant to the day-to-day performance of a small-cap portfolio, clients have no reason to invest in small-cap stocks unless they can beat that index over full market cycles. So, we have two relevant indexes: the market index and the small-cap index.

Reilly: At Putnam Investment Management, we also look at the performance of normal portfolios. In other words, if the computer has the same screens we do, what portfolio does it build, and can we beat that portfolio?

Question: When valuations get too high, do you look at absolute levels or market-relative levels, and how do you define "too high"?

Breed: We look at valuations relative to a corresponding fundamental attribute. Instead of using an iterative screening process to screen out stocks that have no yield or have P/Es of more than 10, 12, or 15 (whatever the market is), we look at valuations in relation to the corresponding fundamental attribute with which they are least correlated.

For example, what company is most likely to be able to increase its dividend, if it has one? The company with the highest cash flow reinvestment rate may decide not to pay a dividend at all. It is going to reinvest that money in the company, which is fine. In the absence of any dividend payment, all else being equal, you would prefer the company with the highest cash flow reinvestment rate. Of two companies with the same price-to-book ratio, you would prefer the one with the highest return on equity. Of two companies growing at the same rate, buy the one with the lowest P/E. Don't look at valuation levels by themselves, either in absolute or relative terms. Look at them in relation to a corresponding fundamental attribute. We try to buy as much growth as we can at a low P/E.

Question: Four of the five sell criteria that Mr. Breed mentioned had a valuation underpinning, but none of the buy criteria did. Do you believe that valuation is relatively unimportant in a buy decision?

Breed: No, I did not list the five best reasons to buy a stock or the five best reasons to sell a stock. The lists were of five good attributes to look for in owning a company and five to avoid. High valuation is something to avoid when you buy a stock. Again, such decisions are joint ones, not mutually exclusive. A company growing at a 40 percent rate is fine if you buy it at 20 times earnings but maybe not so fine if you have to pay 80 times earnings. Again, look at the fundamental attributes in conjunction with the valuation attributes. The screening process is not iterative but, rather, a combination.

Question: Mr. Reilly, you mentioned that if a stock's P/E gets above the market's, it has to go. Are you using estimated earnings or trailing earnings, and if estimated earnings, how far out? Have you looked at the subsequent performance of some of the stocks that you sold based on some of these valuation measures and how much you may have lost by selling those stocks once you got to a market premium?

Reilly: The selling is based on a P/E that looks 12 months out. Not every stock we sell has a lower-than-market P/E, but more than 90 percent do, and we believe that another 5 percent will very shortly. Moreover, the stocks we sell always go down right after we sell them.

Question: What is your typical portfolio turnover? Is there a point at which your clients get uncomfortable with it? Would your strategy change if you had taxable clients?

Breed: Typical portfolio turnover is roughly 70 percent a year. In such a year as 1995, when everything was up 35–40 percent or more, the turnover rate went up because valuations were being dispersed. In such years as 1994, the turnover rate was lower. Clients worry about turnover only when you underperform.

We, too, do not spend a lot of time analyzing what has happened to a stock after we have sold it. What counts is how much money you are making, not how much money you did not make.

Question: Mr. Reilly, you talked about the diversification requirement and the limits on the different sectors in your portfolio. How strictly do you adhere to those limits, and how do you allocate among them? What causes you to change from being at the low end of a weighting to the high end of the weighting?

Reilly: All we really look at in detail are three big sector weightings: 40 percent industrial, 40 percent consumer, and 20 percent interest-sensitive stocks. We started with that diversification scheme because it closely mimics the Russell 2000.

Most managers have some sort of industry or sector bias that results from having only one or two people managing the money. If I am a capital goods analyst, I tend to own lots of capital goods stocks. If I am a consumer analyst, I own a lot of consumer stocks. Most small-cap managers, whether they are growth or value oriented, do not own much in the way of interest-sensitive stocks because they do not know how to follow them. We have six people managing the money, so we know how to follow everything, and we want to be able to use the entire range of sectors. In fact, what we are really saying is that stock picking is more important than sector selection, and we want to be exposed to all major sectors; we do not want to miss a sector because the analyst is a consumer specialist and does not know anything about industrial stocks.

Question: What sorts of specifics do you look for in managements when you are trying to get a sense of how closely aligned they are with shareholders?

Breed: The first and most obvious one is whether they own any stock. What does the stock option package look like? Although the information may be semipublic, most managers are uncomfortable talking about what their salaries were last year. Is the compensation package heavily driven by salary or by incentives related to how the business is doing or how the stock is doing? You would rather see the latter than the former.

Question: Do you have any guidelines as to how much in stock option compensation is too much?

Breed: When we see a stock option policy that dilutes the outstanding shares by more than 5 percent a year, we want to talk to management about it. We will typically vote against stock option

packages that are anything in excess of that amount unless there is a good reason.

Question: How do you avoid buying a value stock too early? Do you avoid orphan stocks and stocks with no coverage? If not, what would make you look at those rather than some with a small amount of coverage?

Reilly: Currently, Putnam manages about $35 billion of value money, and less than $2 billion of that is small-cap value. Fifteen of us work as a team at value investing. Ten years ago, when I became the chief investment officer of the value group, our theme was buy cheap stocks, and we did not care if we were too early. But we realized we were waiting for lightning to strike, and we could beat that simple criterion by looking, in detail, at what was going on inside the company. So, we send the portfolio managers out to see what is going on at a company and talk to its key decision maker—the CEO or the chief financial officer, for example. You can detect what is going on at the company by visiting it, especially if only you and four other people from Wall Street are visiting the company.

There are also other indicators. Take two stocks such as Kennametal and Greenfield Industries. The two companies are in the same industry, but they differ in subtle ways. They are both value stocks, but one is about three times larger than the other. They are both in the machine cutting-tool business. Greenfield reported a disappointing quarter. This quarter has been the slowdown part of this economic cycle, so for a machine cutting-tool company to have a disappointing quarter is normal as long as you can look back and see that over the whole cycle, it has had far above-average growth. Greenfield's stock sells today at a big

discount to Kennametal's because it announced the disappointing quarter and Kennametal did not. If Greenfield had worded its announcement differently, the stocks probably would be trading in tandem, but they are not. Is it too early to buy Greenfield? Not if you are looking at it the way I just described, but it is if you are saying you want to wait until the first or second quarter or earnings surprises, which is where most growth managers are.

For both large-cap and small-cap stocks, managers invest in current earnings momentum whenever that occurs. We are ahead of the current earnings momentum people, but that puts us in such a minority today that it does not bother me at all.

Question: Mr. Breed, you commented that small companies have done less cost cutting than large-cap companies and, therefore, can improve margins going forward. Do you have any concrete evidence that that has actually happened?

Breed: What I meant was that a lot of the profit growth of large-cap companies has come through cost cutting, not that the small-cap companies have not done it or have it ahead of them. What concerns me is that a large proportion of the earnings growth at the large-cap end of the market has come through cost cutting, which by its very nature cannot recur very often.

Question: Within the small-cap value or growth style, is there a certain amount of money that you can handle without starting to see performance suffer?

Reilly: We did a screen for companies with small-cap values by dividend characteristics. A value-weighted portfolio of the 700 stocks that meet our screen would beat the market. So, there are 700 stocks that you could own and beat the market. The capacity constraint is whether you can actively manage that many stocks. Trimming when they are going up and adding when they are going down takes some flexibility. We have found that getting the process and the methodology right is much more important than trading exactly right or getting the right price for the stock.

Most portfolio managers underperform the market because they are so busy looking in the rearview mirror at what just worked and are chasing that. They have to have the liquidity to get into what just worked and to get out of whatever did not just work. Liquidity is an overblown question that people worry about only when they are underperforming. These styles go in waves. During the past three years, the difference in returns between large-cap growth managers and large-cap value managers has been practically zero. Did they all get the same smarts at the same time? No, the two styles have had a lot of overlapping names in them, especially during the past three years. Such companies as Hewlett Packard Company, IBM Corporation, and Xerox Corporation have bounced back and forth between value and growth, but they have led the market and beaten it for the past three years. Growth and value on the big-cap side look identical; on the small-cap side, they look very different, but that is because of the style, not the activity, of the manager.

Breed: There has been market-capitalization creep, so the definition of small cap has changed. Along with that change, the amount of aggregate assets you can manage has changed. Regardless of what the definition of small cap is, the smallest cap stock that would qualify to be included in your portfolio ultimately determines your liquidity constraint. You do not want to own more than 5 percent of the outstanding stock of a $100 million-cap company. Otherwise, you have reporting requirements, liquidity problems, and all the rest. If you put 5 percent of a $100 million market-cap stock in your portfolio, then you should not be managing more than $500 million in assets or the holding will not count. The low end of what you define as small cap is what ultimately causes liquidity constraints.

Question: Many small-cap companies have no earnings. Do you exclude them from your evaluation screens?

Reilly: In screening for low P/E, which we do, it is hard for a company with no earnings to squeeze through, but we do make exceptions; for example, companies can have write-offs or a bad earnings year. We have been over this universe so many times, however, that if something new comes in that looks as if it fits—it has had a write-off or bad earnings year—but we have never seen it before, then we are probably a bit skeptical. If it is a company we have known for the past ten years, one bad year will not exclude it from our screen.

Breed: If a low P/E is good, is a negative P/E better? We use expected earnings rather than trailing earnings in our screens. Analysts are an optimistic lot, and no one expects companies to have negative earnings, so the problem becomes one of overoptimistic expectations rather than the company having trailing earnings that were either zero or less. Interestingly, through the first six months of 1996, the stocks that did the best were stocks with no trailing earnings at all.

Question: For a small-cap value manager, what are the risks of investing in slow-growing companies? Is there a limit to the portfolio return you can expect over time and to how much P/E expansion you can add to the underlying returns?

Reilly: When the market's investment focus narrows to one or two anointed industries, which we saw in 1993, 1995, and 1996, then it is difficult for someone who is very diversified to keep up. It is also difficult to keep up when people are willing to pay some infinite valuation for stocks that have anticipated earnings but nothing in the current time period.

Styles come and go in waves. When people are pessimistic, as they were in 1988 and 1990, value looks great. In periods of optimism, as in 1993, 1995, and the beginning of 1996, value stinks. So, you have to take the long-term view. Nobody wants to buy based on two-year or even three-year records because if you have beaten the market for three years, the chances of your beating the market for the next three years are low, and vice versa. Of course, most plan sponsors screen on who has just done well. That practice is the same as buying stocks when they have just gone up a lot. I want the manager who is hot. I want the stock that is hot.

We believe you need a small-cap value manager and a small-cap growth manager, just as you need a large-cap growth manager and a large-cap value manager, because it is hard to predict when which style is going to work. So, we have exposure in each category.

Question: In working with clients to determine benchmarks, what kind of investment horizon do you use for the fund's performance versus the benchmark?

Breed: We all talk about full market cycles, so the horizon depends on how you define a market cycle, peak to peak or trough to trough. Most of our clients recognize that 12 months is too short a time frame. If you do not start off with a positive performance, however, no one is going to hang around with you for five years, so we are happy with rolling three-year time frames, and our clients seem to be happy with that. This time frame seems to be a good middle point and something everybody can define up front.

Reilly: For comparison purposes, we array the performance of all mutual fund small-cap value managers. This array is much more readily available than looking at institutional databases. We look back at their performance because we have had a small-cap product out since the beginning of 1988. Three years ago, more than half of such managers had beaten the Russell 2000. Today, just a handful do. Clearly, something has happened in the past three or so years that has made it almost impossible for a small-cap value manager to beat the market, which is exactly the opposite of the trend in 1988, 1989, and 1990, when most small-cap value managers were beating the market.

Three years is probably too short a time frame, although most people look at that as the minimum. Much more important is taking a look at the normal portfolio. Are you adding value to that in, say, three years? If not, then maybe that portfolio needs to be rebalanced.

Question: The difference between Putnam I and II is that Putnam I has a dividend requirement and Putnam II does not, but both are value oriented. Do either or both of them use convertibles, and how have these two value styles performed versus some of

Putnam's small-cap growth funds?

Reilly: By not requiring a dividend, you get companies that are smaller, a little less mature, and a little faster growing than the average company. They are closer in growth rate to our small-cap growth portfolios, and although there is almost no overlap between our small-cap value portfolio and our small-cap growth portfolio, the growth rates and valuations are close. Their performance is highly correlated, too. In the past three years, our Small-Cap II has beaten our Small-Cap I, and the Small-Cap I acts a lot like the more conservative of the other mutual funds. All the value products at Putnam are defined as value by being less risky than the market, whether it is the Russell 2000 or the S&P 500. All the growth products are defined as being more risky than the market; our Small-Cap II portfolio is close in risk to the Russell 2000, and therefore, it is getting borderline toward where the growth funds are.

Question: No one has mentioned market timing. What sort of cash levels do you maintain? How do you modify them? Do you agree that a lot of fund manager performance is a result of being in and out of the market at just the right or wrong time?

Breed: I am not good at market timing and do not do it. We try to maintain cash positions of less than 5 percent, across all our portfolios. One analysis showed that if you took the entire market rise over the past 20 years and just missed the best 40 days, you would wind up doing no better than T-bills! Unfortunately, I have never gotten a call in advance of one of those 40 days telling me I'd better get invested for tomorrow. I doubt that market

timing can be done with any kind of repeatability.

Question: To what extent do you buy stocks not covered by any analysts at all?

Reilly: Stocks like that are hard to find today, but they do not all have the same amount and degree of coverage. The regional brokers have somebody they call their small-cap value analyst or their small-cap value team, and they usually cover a laundry list of names, so they talk to the companies less often than we do.

Breed: What we define as small cap today is, in effect, an overlay for the Russell 2000. Very few companies are not covered at all. They may not be covered by Wall Street, but they are covered by regional brokers. Among the microcaps—stocks under $100 million in market cap—a fair number of companies have no earnings estimates, but we would look at them for our microcap product.

Question: Where are we in the relative performance cycle of small- versus large-cap stocks?

Reilly: The most important step perhaps is to take apart the Russell 2000 and take apart the S&P 500 and see where the big industry bets are and where the performance cycles come from. I do not want to overstate this process, because technology in small cap does not behave exactly like technology in large cap, but they have a high degree of correlation. For example, technology has about 30 percent higher weighting in the Russell 2000 than in the S&P 500. Health care is not so different. Capital goods in total are much higher in the S&P 500 than in the Russell 2000, but banks have much more weight in the Russell 2000. You are really looking at waves of performance in certain sectors within the two indexes, not necessarily small cap versus large cap.

Breed: I am concerned that Claudia Mott proclaimed the death of the current cycle, which has lasted only three years.[1] Perhaps that means it started in the third quarter of 1990 and ended at the end of 1993. I am not sure there is any magic to that five-plus-year cycle. Clearly, if there were, we would still be in an up cycle, which has not been the case for the past two or more years. Look at the relative valuations of the small- and

[1]See Ms. Mott's presentation, pp. 4–7.

large-cap ends of the market. We are not at the bottom of the outperformance of large-cap stocks, but we may be at the start of a new small-cap cycle.

Question: Do you have any guidelines about how long a company has to be public before you will buy? Many that come out disappoint after a couple of quarters and become value stocks. Is that an entry point?

Breed: Although we do not have a specific policy against buying initial public offerings (IPOs), we prefer not to do so. The idea in an IPO is to get top dollar, not bottom, for the sellers, so we are skeptical

when it comes to buying them.

Nothing is magical about how long it takes for a post-IPO stock to become reasonably valued. As an example, Callaway Golf Company is a stock that we bought post-IPO. It nearly doubled on the day it became public and then traded down for six months until it got back to its IPO price, when we bought it. There is no particular magic to a specific period of time, but you want to avoid the stocks for which extremely high valuations, in terms of price-to-book or price-to-earnings ratios, were accorded on the day they became public.

Quantitative Methods in Managing Small-Cap Portfolios

Daniel N. Ginsparg
Vice President
Boatmen's Trust Company

Quantitative research is an essential part of small-cap investing, but because many small-cap stocks are underfollowed, reliable information on them is hard to obtain.

This presentation provides a brief overview of how to produce relevant investment sets. The emphasis is on how to use an investment process that relies on objective evaluation techniques without attempting to differentiate quantitative from fundamental information, because almost everything analysts do is based on fundamental information.

OBJECTIVITY

Because emotion can play a major role in small-cap investing, the need for objectivity becomes critical. For example, if you play golf but dislike Callaway Golf Company clubs, you are unlikely to buy stock in the company. Unlike large, diversified firms with multiple products, small firms generally have a very small range of products and are easily identified with those products. Objective investment techniques help to remove emotion from investment decisions.

Another example of keeping emotion in check is an experience we had with Dollar General Corporation. We bought this stock based on our analysis, which identified the company as a compelling buy opportunity. During the period that we owned Dollar General shares, I happened to pass by one of their stores. I figured we owned the stock so I should go in and see what the store looks like. I was astounded. To me, it looked like a junk store. Clearly, I was not the target market. If my emotions had come into play, I would have sold the shares, but looking at it objectively allowed me to see that it was a well-managed cash machine. We stayed the course, and our investment in Dollar General performed extremely well.

WHY SMALL-CAP STOCKS

An analyst trying to identify a superior investment opportunity must first determine where to look. If the universe is too small, then opportunities are often overlooked. The larger the universe gets, however, the more cumbersome it becomes to work with. The size of the potential universe grows significantly larger as you move down the capitalization spectrum. With thousands of companies to choose from, new opportunities constantly present themselves. Without some form of objective search technique, sifting through all of the rapidly changing information is almost impossible. By always looking through this large universe, you can maintain a portfolio that is growing faster than the average company without pursuing extreme valuations. This portfolio produces higher returns with considerably less risk than the usual portfolio, because you can avoid holding companies for which expectations have reached an extreme.

BUILDING A MODEL

The first step in building a model that can assist in the analysis of small-cap companies is to explore and learn as much as possible about this sector. With the knowledge you develop, you can synthesize what you believe are the critical variables leading to success.

Our firm has developed a process that combines forecasting company fundamentals with analyst expectations about those fundamentals. We also use traditional valuation analysis to pare down the list of investable small-cap companies. We are big proponents of multifactor modeling, or looking at more than one variable at a time. Single-factor models tend to produce more volatility than multifactor models because they fail to take more than one influential factor into account. By considering three or four factors, each component can provide additional information while reducing the volatility of the portfolio the model creates.

©Association for Investment Management and Research

Data Collection

An essential step when developing an objective investment process is data collection. Before an identified investment process can be backtested to see if it is valid, clean and pertinent data must be gathered. Many data sets are available that provide company-specific financial and accounting information. Standard & Poor's Compustat is the most widely known and used database of financial information. For historical and forecast earnings estimates, good databases are available from Zacks Investment Research, I/B/E/S International, and First Call Corporation.

Although many of these agencies provide reliable data, analysts should perform several confirmation activities to ensure the integrity of the data. The first problem you will encounter is that each firm usually handles historical ticker symbols differently. If an analyst is not careful, Security Pacific Corporation, whose ticker was SPC, becomes St. Paul Companies, whose current ticker is SPC. Clearly, this exchange will have a dramatic effect on the backtest results. Analysts should try to develop their own unique identifiers or use a reliable source such as the CRSP unique identifier.

Another related issue is that of data storage. Data generally come in a relational format; that is, each company is listed along with its ticker symbol and some financial information or earnings estimates. To build an investment process, you must analyze this information across time. Thus, the data are in three dimensions and should be stored in a manner that allows the development of a relational time series. Sybase Limited and Oracle Corporation are two companies with software packages that can store data this way for relatively easy access.

The most important aspect of data confirmation, however, is checking for missing data and data anomalies. An out-of-place decimal point can dramatically influence the backtesting results. For instance, an earnings estimate of $3.25 that is stored as $32.50 will create severe estimation problems, especially in working with small data sets. Related problems include incorrect split adjustments and outright gaps in the data. We attempt to capture and correct as many of these problems as possible before proceeding to use the data.

Data Use Problems

Once you have collected a fairly clean data set, you still need to modify the data to make them relevant before you start building your investment process. You will first want to address issues regarding the time sequencing of the data, especially as you compare fiscal with calendar periods. You may also want to modify the data because of issues relating to the scale of the data.

Scale refers to the relative degree of change. How important is a 10 cent change? For an earnings estimate, a 10 cent change is much more critical for a company expected to earn $0.30 than it is for a company whose earnings are expected to be $3.00. The same pattern applies when considering a stock price change. A $1.00 change in a $10.00 stock is a 10 percent move, yet $1.00 represents only a 1 percent move for a $100.00 stock. These differences in scale have to be considered and adjusted for when analyzing stocks—particularly small-cap stocks.

Time-sequencing adjustment, or calendarization, is required when you are using data that are released on a fiscal basis but used on a calendar basis. For example, assume that your model requires a three-month estimate. At the very beginning of a fiscal quarter, you have a pure three-month-ahead estimate to use in your model. A month later, however, you have only a two-month estimate. If the model still requires a three-month estimate, you have to somehow combine two quarterly estimates to form the required input.

An even more critical time issue occurs at the end of a quarter before the company reports. At this time, you have an estimate for the quarter just ended and you have next quarter's estimate. You will have to develop a methodology to deal with this critical juncture. If you truncate the old estimate, you may lose vital information as analysts make final changes to this number in the days leading up to the announcement date. If you use both pieces of data in their entirety, however, then exactly what are you measuring at that point? The resolution of these time calendarization and scale modification issues is critical before attempting to evaluate historical data.

Model Testing

We have now arrived at the backtest stage of the process, which is probably one of the most-abused procedures. In fact, the usual advice is to "go in there and torture the data until it confesses." By pounding away at the data, eventually you will find something that has worked in the past. The problem is whether that solution is truly relevant and whether it can be replicated in the future.

The entire testing phase is a learning experience. The way I like to think of it is that you start out with a goal, such as putting a screw into a wall. You might reach into your toolbox, and the first thing you pull out is a hammer. There is no question that you can put the screw into the wall with the hammer. Having tested this with gratifying results, you would quit testing and proceed to put all of your screws in the wall with a hammer. You might even accept the occasional shortfall that occurs when you miss, thus putting large holes into the wall beside your screws.

The other strategy is to turn your toolbox upside down and empty all of your tools out onto the floor. Then, after carefully thinking about how you would use each tool, you decide that the screwdriver is the best tool to try. You try it, and it works. You may try the hammer for comparison, but you select the screwdriver because it lacks the shortfall risk. You may even pick up your drill and predrill a hole, thus implementing a multifactor strategy that provides even better results.

This type of testing is what we advocate. Start by carefully defining the problem you are trying to solve and then look objectively at all of your available tools. Use the entire process as a learning experience. Try the hammer but be sure to stay objective and evaluate whether or not you have found the best solution. If your backtest is thorough, it will examine each period and identify what is going on in the economy and at the individual-firm level.

When we develop investment techniques, we try to use a backtest methodology that allows the analyst freedom to learn about what is influencing the companies at both the macro and the micro levels. We avoid the usual test of seeing how well a specific variable explains historical returns. We usually start with a broad definition of what we are going to explore, such as "how best to put a screw into a wall" or, specifically, "the sensitivity of the prices of small companies to changes in profitability."

We have found that the majority of small companies are what we call "fallen angels," or mid- to large-capitalization companies that, for various reasons, are now much smaller. We may want to test to see if the prices of these fallen angels are more sensitive than others to changes in operating profitability or gross profitability. Maybe they are equally sensitive to both profitability measures, because by definition, they have undergone a significant downsizing.

We try to isolate the effects of the economy and understand how it is influencing our results. We would also examine these companies at the industry or sector level. Companies rarely demonstrate the same level of sensitivity in all industries. The teaching point here is that backtests should provide analysts with opportunities to learn about what they are exploring and to examine the effects of every tool in their tool boxes. You should not perform backtests merely to fit models to historic data in the hope that the patterns you have found will continue to work in the future.

Another important aspect of a backtest is to identify and study when and why a model is not working. Everybody likes to talk about success when things work. What is also required is to understand why a model is not working and to determine the shortfall risks to any strategy. You should explore the dynamics of your model over all time periods and determine the magnitude of any shortfall whenever it occurs.

Designing Better Backtesting

Typically, you have a limited number of data points with which to run backtests. If you are lucky, your data set will have 20 years of monthly data, or 240 data points. Unfortunately, this set leaves you with a very time-dependent, small series to work with as compared with the statistical modeling performed in other disciplines.

One way to improve these data sets is to use a bootstrapping methodology. Bootstrapping gives you the capability of expanding the use of your data. With bootstrapping, you randomly select periods from within a particular data set and test your model. You will probably find variables in your model that validate for one random period but not for other periods. This procedure also helps remove the sensitivity of your backtest to when your data set begins. Bootstrapping is a way to extend the use of your data and thus produce more reliable backtests. This ability to remove the time dependence of most backtests is critical and leads to more robust results.

Most people who backtest select holdout samples to validate their models. The holdout sample may be either a slice of time or a slice of the universe. Analysts fit their models using the majority of the data available and then validate using these slices. Using a time slice approach causes problems, however, because most time periods encompass unique information that may not recur. Universe segmentation is more reliable if you have sufficient data.

To create these universe slices, you must stratify your universe into segments that contain companies with similar characteristics. If you have properly constructed these subuniverses, you then have two slices that should include similar sensitivity to time. You may then fit your models to one of the segments and validate it using the other segment. No method is perfect, but if you have a large enough universe to start with, then segmentation is usually a more reliable technique.

When designing a better backtest, stay cognizant of two biases that can slip into the process: survivor bias and look-ahead bias. Survivor bias is the result of companies disappearing from the data set. Regardless of which of the previously mentioned techniques you use, you must ensure that all companies are in your database for the period you are testing, even if they no longer exist. Depending upon what you are testing, these outlier companies can heavily influence backtest results.

Look-ahead bias results from having the advantage of hindsight. Make sure the data you are testing look as close as possible to the way the world really was and what was readily available at the time the data were gathered. Sometimes you cannot get away from look-ahead bias. One way to examine the effect of look-ahead bias on your backtest is to lag variables, thus penalizing the information.

For example, you think that the estimates you are examining were not fully known at the time reflected in the database. You can lag this information and make it available one to two months later than your database says it was available. Test this lagged data and see what it does to your results. If the value of the information drops off quickly, you may want to reevaluate your original results.

PORTFOLIO SELECTION

Once you have tested and fine-tuned your model, you are ready to select a portfolio of stocks. In this step of the process, you might reduce the number of companies in the investable universe from as many as 4,000 to 5,000 into a more manageable set. Normally, if a reliable time series is required, you can find sufficient clean data on about 1,500–2,000 small-cap companies. The model should have a set of rules that can be used to reduce this number even more. For example: Remove any company for which gross revenues are declining. Applying well-researched theory is important at this point. Remember, to use a repeatable and consistent strategy that avoids data mining, you must always have a clear idea of what you are looking for.

If all of the previous steps were successful, you should have an attractive short list of small-cap securities. At this point, you may perform some limited subjective analysis to help you make that final buy or sell determination. Our objective approach does not preclude subjective analysis, it helps us to focus on the most recent compelling ideas. In addition, it provides a discipline that helps us to overcome the emotion that usually accompanies most investment decisions.

TRADING AND EXECUTION

Trading and execution is without a doubt one of the most important aspects of the entire small-cap investment process. Commissions are not the issue; the real trading cost is the change in price caused by executing more shares than the market is willing to transact. Although this price impact happens occasionally

when trading large-cap companies, it happens consistently when trading small-cap companies.

We spend a lot of time focusing on trading and execution. Assume, for example, that turnover is 70 percent and transaction costs are 6 percent on a round-trip basis. If you can get that 6 percent down to 3 percent, your performance will be enhanced by 210 basis points.

We try to find a balance between the speed we need to put an idea to work and the amount of market impact we are willing to absorb. Patience can often help. In some particular names, we may be willing to be very patient. We work to get a better understanding of how transaction costs are going to affect a particular stock or company. Our overriding concern is the fact that in the small-cap world, success is rewarded immensely but failure is heavily penalized. When an idea does not work out, the cost of getting out of that security may be more than you could possibly lose on the stock if you just held it.

The liquidity of one stock often can be used to offset the illiquidity of another. This aspect is where we have extended our utility function beyond the usual trade-off for an individual security. This approach allows us to maximize our alpha while minimizing transaction costs. To own every stock that is attractive may result in a portfolio that is too expensive to purchase. We have found that a somewhat similar portfolio is available that does not include every security but still has much of the sensitivity and return potential of the ideal portfolio.

CONCLUSION

Subjecting the universe of 4,000 or more small-cap firms to a rigorous bottom-up analysis is both time and cost prohibitive. Nevertheless, you can identify several characteristics that you feel represent the type of company you want to own and then test to determine whether these characteristics are actually related to future increases in security prices. Using these objective measures and the power of technology, you can reduce this enormous universe to a smaller and more workable list without missing any new opportunity. This list should represent the "best of the best." You may want to further analyze the entire list and reduce it to the one or two new companies you wish to add to your portfolio. This analysis then feeds into portfolio construction, which is heavily influenced by trading costs. The desired result should be an outperforming portfolio of small-cap stocks.

Question and Answer Session

Daniel N. Ginsparg

Question: Can you suggest one or more good backtesting software packages?

Ginsparg: We could not find one that suited our needs, so we built our own. Some good ones are available, however: FactSet Research Systems has a good one, as does Zacks. When I was using them, I spent so much time preparing the data to go into the program, the process became very cumbersome and hard to track. Also, I like to analyze things graphically, especially checking for changes and analyzing extreme conditions. I have not found a package that allows you to do that very flexibly.

Question: In looking through databases, do you try to identify nonrecurring income and expense items and adjust earnings accord-ingly? Also, do you try to identify R&D or other strategic transformation expenses?

Ginsparg: No, we do not. The cost of doing that ourselves would be astronomical. Most of the historical databases are supposed to provide clean operating earnings, but probably that is not always true. The idea is to be consistent, especially when handling operating earnings. Another good idea is to use several of the database services to compare them for accuracy. Historically, we have tended to stick with one database—Zacks. Zacks tends to do a very good job of cleaning out nonrecurring items from quarterly earnings.

Question: After the quantitative process is completed, you mentioned that security analysis is the next step. How in-depth and at what level of detail is this analysis being completed?

Ginsparg: We have built tools to look at companies on an individual basis, and we do talk to analysts, but the majority of what we do is based on our objective process. By the time we get to this point in the process, we are pretty comfortable with the securities that are being considered.

Question: Do you buy non-Nasdaq OTC stocks?

Ginsparg: No, we do not do that because of the lack of really good information available on those securities and the fact that very few analysts actually follow them.

Unique Issues in Small-Cap and Microcap Portfolio Management

Peter C. Schliemann
Executive Vice President
David L. Babson & Company, Inc.

The small- and microcap universes are subject to tremendous flux. The turnover on the Russell 2000 Index is more than double that on the S&P 500 Index. This variability makes the research function extremely important, yet very difficult. From a fundamental perspective, lack of product and customer depth and breadth and limited corporate resources (both financial and management) challenge the research effort. Illiquidity, high transaction costs, and encumbering filing requirements further complicate portfolio management for small- and microcap sectors.

Small- and microcap securities are hard to define from the point of view of capitalization because the classification range is constantly changing. The average capitalization in the Russell 2000 Index of small-cap stocks has more than doubled in the past three years; the largest company in the index now exceeds $1 billion in capitalization. The ceiling for the CRSP 9–10, which is used to benchmark microcap securities, has increased from $81 million in market capitalization in 1991 to $197 million currently.

With a sector that is in a state of constant revaluation, how does a money manager come up with new investment ideas? The decision-making process involves both research and analysis. Research uncovers facts, and analysis uses those facts to generate good investments. With large-cap securities, the research aspect is fairly minimal. A whole host of Wall Street and regional brokerage firms have researched those companies from all angles. Because almost everything relevant has already been uncovered, the job of the large-cap investor is mostly analyzing that information to make investment decisions. Probably 80 percent of the effort with large-cap investing is spent on analysis and 20 percent on research.

For small- and microcap stocks, the research function requires greater effort than the analytical function. Wall Street coverage of small-cap firms is very limited, and much of the relevant information has to be selectively dug out. Even regional houses do not cover all the companies, so great emphasis is placed on digging up the facts. With microcap stocks, the primary and most difficult task is finding information about a company. Information on large-cap companies is available in most databases, but very few microcap companies are carried in the databases.

The challenge is made more difficult because the small size deciles contain many more companies than do the larger size deciles, and the turnover among companies in the small deciles is greater. The universe of large companies in the S&P 500 Index is clearly smaller in number than the 2,000 small companies in the Russell 2000. The universe of microcap companies is huge; thousands of companies are in these very small market-cap ranges.

The constant turnover makes keeping up with firms in the small- and microcap sectors even more difficult. Seventy-seven percent of companies listed in the S&P 500 five years ago are still there, compared with only 32 percent in the Russell 2000. Worse, only 18.5 percent of the companies in the Russell 2000 today were in it 10 years ago. The number of new companies added to the Russell 2000 in 1996 was close to a record. About a quarter of that index is new each year, and a third of the companies have fewer than four years of trading history. The successful firms move up in capitalization, but many move down and eventually disappear.

RESEARCH

The research function in the small- and microcap sectors is very different from that for large-cap securities. Few analysts actively cover smaller companies, which results in a substantial information gap. **Figure 1** breaks down Compustat data to show the

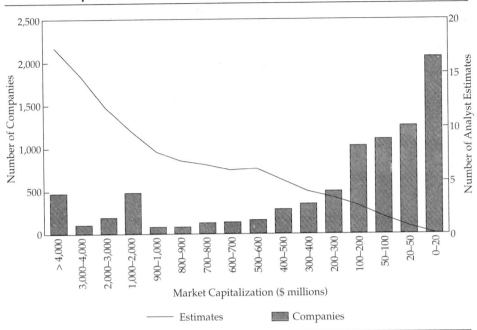

Sources: FactSet Research Systems; I/B/E/S International.

range of analyst coverage for various market capitalizations. The 500 or so companies with capitalizations greater than $4 billion are covered by about 17 analysts per company. The two smallest size groups, firms with capitalizations of less than $50 million, which is clearly microcap, collectively have about 3,500 companies, but virtually no analysts cover firms smaller than $20 million, and only 0.7 analysts per company cover the $20 million to $50 million category.

Clearly, Wall Street is not actively covering many of the small-sized firms. Analysts and portfolio managers interested in these sectors must be willing to do most of the in-depth research themselves. In many cases, they will be the only ones doing any research on a firm, and often, they will be the first to look at the company. Such researchers require independence and confidence in their research, because very little comparable information is available with which to verify and validate their work.

Relative to their larger counterparts, small firms must be analyzed in a more dynamic and higher risk environment. Compared with a large company that is broadly diversified and has a professional management team, for small-cap and microcap companies have much greater risks. Small-cap and microcap companies tend to be one-product companies that sell to a narrow list of customers. If a product becomes obsolete or a customer has problems, a small company does not always have the financial staying power to keep afloat.

The quality of management is vastly different between large and small firms. Most microcap companies are run by their founders and have no "professional" management. As these companies grow, the demands on management can change quickly, and many of the entrepreneur managers cannot make that transition. From an accessibility and information-quality viewpoint, talking directly with the CEO is easier and provides more reliable information than other sources, but that environment is difficult and high risk. Analysts and portfolio managers must be able to distance themselves emotionally from a firm, although in many cases, they get to know the CEO and the company fairly intimately. Often, they are the first to uncover a company, which may create a sense of ownership and make that stock very difficult to part with when the time comes to sell.

PORTFOLIO MANAGEMENT

Once the research has been done and the ideas developed, the next step is to put them together into a portfolio. Stocks of large companies can often be purchased within a matter of hours by going to the trading desk or calling a broker. Buying a small-cap stock may take weeks or months because the market has very few open positions for these stocks. This scarcity often leads to large price effects because of efforts to encourage positions on the sell side.

The illiquidity of small-cap stocks is evident from the bid–ask spread on stocks traded on Nasdaq. For stocks of companies with market capitalizations exceeding $250 million, the bid–ask spread average is 1.4 percent; for stocks of companies of less than $25 million, the spread is 6.9 percent; and even in the $50 million to $100 million capitalization range, a reasonably popular one, the spread is about 4 percent. These spreads are generally for small orders—100 shares or so. For large order sizes, the bid–ask spread is even wider. Crossing networks is a helpful solution to this problem.

As **Figure 2** illustrates, sometimes waiting and being patient in executing a trade can provide bid and ask prices much closer than the stated spread, but waiting too long is also a problem. The opportunity costs associated with losing the informational advantage to other analysts may be extremely high.

Figure 2. Transaction Costs

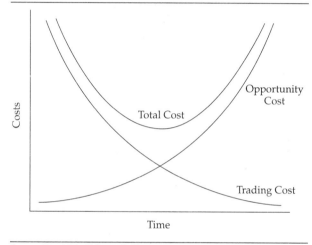

Source: David L. Babson & Company.

PORTFOLIO SIZE

An issue that can have serious implications in the construction of a small- or microcap portfolio is the amount of assets an investor wants to own. The amount of assets held depends on the number of companies owned, the desired percentage of ownership in each company, and the average market capitalization. Passive managers can own literally hundreds of companies, but active managers cannot because they are limited by the resources they can expend on the analysis necessary for active management. A small active management firm will have a hard time following 100 companies closely. Adequate portfolio diversification is not really an issue with small-cap stocks. Most managers are limited by not wanting to own too many companies.

The percentage ownership desired in each com-

pany depends largely on an individual manager's own comfort level and tolerance with SEC filing requirements and the need for liquidity. Obviously, an investor can own a substantial share in small companies for a lot less capital than for the same share in larger companies, which can trigger regulatory filings. The SEC requires that Schedule 13D be filed by "any person or group acquiring 'beneficial ownership' of more than 5 percent of a class of equity security" within 10 days of the acquisition that brought the ownership above 5 percent. Certain institutional investors buying stock in the ordinary course of business and not acquiring stock to influence control over the company may submit a modified schedule (Schedule 13G), which changes the filing deadline to 45 days after the end of the calendar year in which ownership exceeded 5 percent. This form must also be filed within 10 days after the end of the month in which ownership exceeds 10 percent. Many portfolio managers find these filing requirements onerous, and their tolerance for them may dictate how much stock of a particular company they want to own.

Investors' liquidity considerations are also important. For those who need to have their hands on their money quickly, owning a large percentage of each company can be a serious mistake. Reversing a large position in a small company can be extremely difficult and also extremely costly. Ownership stakes can be higher when the client has a long investment horizon.

The ownership issue also depends on how actively a portfolio manager wants to be involved in the activities of a company. Shareholder activism can easily become an issue, especially in a microcap environment. Dealing with underperforming managements and fighting against poison pills and other impediments to takeovers can be quite time-consuming.

CONCLUSION

Benjamin Graham, in an article in the *Financial Analysts Journal* about 20 years ago, said that he had pretty much given up on being able to use research to uncover superior investment ideas.[1] This statement is not true for small- and microcap investing. It is the one frontier of investing in which good fundamental research can still add value. That is why investing in these stocks is the most gratifying job in this industry.

[1] "A Conversation with Benjamin Graham," September/October 1976:20–23.

Question and Answer Session

Peter C. Schliemann

Question: Are on-site visits with companies more important when researching small-cap as opposed to large-cap companies?

Schliemann: On-site visits are necessary, especially for one-product, one-plant companies. Beyond that, talking with the customers of and suppliers to those companies is critical. Talking with 30–40 people is not unusual for us in our due diligence when looking at a company. To avoid a bias, most of the people we talk with are company outsiders. The customers are probably the best source of information because they are the first to know about problems with a product or about new competitors.

Question: You mentioned that buying many companies is probably best, but does overdiversification (too many stocks) hurt performance?

Schliemann: Overdiversification does make a portfolio become more and more like an index. If you are able to add value in this sector, you do not want to have that value dissipate by owning 200–300 companies.

Question: Why do trading costs drop through time? Commissions and bid–ask spreads do not shrink over the course of a trade, do they?

Schliemann: Trading costs decline over time because, even though the spread itself does not change, where within that spread you buy the stock is influenced by being patient. If you need to buy the stock on the first day, you are likely to pay a premium over the ask price, but if you are willing to be patient, you can often buy at the midpoint of the spread.

Question: Is there an optimal number of names that a small-cap or microcap analyst can follow?

Schliemann: I cannot give you an optimal number, but if you are the only one digging up information and analyzing it, covering many companies is going to be arduous. Many microcap analysts have told me that covering more than 40 companies is difficult. In analyzing a relatively homogeneous industry, such as the banking industry, which has hundreds of publicly traded companies, some analysts may be comfortable following a lot more than 40 companies. Because a lot of information is readily available for large-cap firms, an analyst could probably cover 100 of them without much difficulty.

Question: Relative to a large-cap value product, how much higher are fees for small-cap and microcap funds?

Schliemann: Fees are higher compared with those of large-cap funds because of the effort that goes into the research. On average, microcap managers charge about 150 basis points (bps) and small-cap managers, about 100 bps; most large-cap managers find that getting much more than 50–75 bps is difficult.

Question: Do you use computer screening to cull through the huge universes of microcap securities for your ideas?

Schliemann: We do have a screening process, but for microcaps, many of the screens do not have enough information and, in many cases, do not even have the companies. I like the William O'Neil database. Although some of these databases can be outrageously expensive for a one-person shop, they have a great deal of information on companies of all sizes. Obviously, a passive approach that uses only screens can be popular in microcap because it is a lot easier and less expensive than staffing up to analyze each holding rigorously.

Question: Are the analysts who work on your team specialists with particular industry assignments or are they generalists?

Schliemann: They are mostly generalists, because microcap companies rarely fit neatly into industries or sectors. Many are almost industries unto themselves. The process should allow for research on almost any company without classification into an industry because, in essence, the companies have very similar issues: management, product depth and breadth, and customer breadth.

International Small-Cap Investing

Daniel L. Jacobs, CFA
President
Jacobs Asset Management

Small-cap stocks outperform their large-cap counterparts in international markets. This outperformance is drawing considerable investor attention, and new indexes dedicated to international small-caps are currently being developed. This presentation discusses the attractions and difficulties of investing in international small-cap stocks.

International small-capitalization stocks are an evolving asset class with little historical data or experience to offer. Only recently have dedicated indexes for international small-cap stocks been developed. This presentation examines three questions pertaining to international small-cap stocks: Do small-cap stocks outperform large-cap stocks internationally? Will international small-cap stocks become a distinct asset class? Is now a good time to invest in international small-cap stocks?

The answer to all three questions is yes. The small-cap effect, in which small-cap stocks outperform their larger-cap counterparts on a risk-adjusted basis, has drawn increased attention from investors, and with the development of new benchmark indexes, international small-cap stocks will soon be an accepted asset class. These stocks are also undervalued currently, so the investment climate appears right for investing in them.

THE INTERNATIONAL SMALL-CAP EFFECT

Evidence of the existence of an international small-cap effect is provided in **Table 1,** which shows annual compound returns and standard deviations for large and small international stocks. The large-cap stocks, represented by the MSCI Europe/Australia/Far East (EAFE) Index, have risen by about 16 percent annually during the past 20 years. In contrast, the small international stocks have risen at an annual rate of about 23 percent, clearly outperforming the large stocks.

The statistics in Table 1 are from a study by Rex Sinquefeld, who shows that investing in international developed markets may not be profitable unless the investments are in value and small-cap stocks, because that is where the inefficiencies are. Sinquefeld also shows the diversification benefits of using international small-cap stocks. During the 1975–94 period, a strictly domestic portfolio earned almost 13 percent compounded annually and had a standard deviation of about 10 percent. A portfolio that included 15 percent international small-cap stocks increased the return to 14.5 percent, almost 2 percent better than investing in the United States alone, and it reduced the standard deviation to 9.4 percent. Another portfolio with an even greater proportion of international small-cap and value stocks earned a return of 15.6 percent, with the same standard deviation as the U.S.-only portfolio. Thus, Sinquefeld makes a compelling case for adding international small-cap and value stocks to domestic portfolios. Sinquefeld's study does not include emerging markets; clearly, the international portfolios would have done much better had emerging markets been included.

The relative outperformance of small-cap stocks in developed and emerging markets is reinforced by the return data in **Tables 2** and **3.** Table 2 shows cap-weighted and equal-weighted returns (in U.S. dollars) for large- and small-cap stocks in developed markets. Cap-weighted return calculations allow larger countries, such as Japan, to have a higher weighting than the smaller countries. The table shows that during the 1989–95 period, small-cap returns compounded over the seven years at 3 percent, compared with 1.6 percent for the large-cap stocks. That differential is not inspiring. Why go international to get 3 percent over seven years? The poor performance during the past seven years of a very prominent market such as Japan may explain this poor performance.

The lower panel of Table 2 shows the same data on an equal-weight basis—that is, Japan, say, has the same weight as Hong Kong or Italy. The returns grew much faster on this basis than cap-weighted returns, while the difference between large- and small-cap returns was smaller—only 1 percent difference.

Table 1. The International Small-Cap Effect

	1970–94		1975–94		
Statistic	Large (EAFE)	Small	Large (EAFE)	Value (large and small)	Small
Compound return	13.2	20.9	16.3	22.3	23.3
Standard deviation	23.4	31.5	22.0	23.0	28.5

Source: Rex Sinquefield, "Where Are the Gains from International Diversification?" *Financial Analysts Journal* (January/February 1996): 8–14.

A list showing the developed countries where large-cap and small-cap stocks outperformed is given in **Exhibit 1**. The list is based on Wilshire Associates data for the past seven years.

One country to note is the United Kingdom, where large-cap stocks outperformed small-cap stocks. The United Kingdom is about the most dangerous place for investing in small caps. Apparently, entrepreneurs in the United Kingdom have no trouble getting capital, which tends to encourage riskier ventures. The result is numerous blow-ups among small-cap companies.

The situation in emerging markets is very different. Table 3 shows that on a cap-weighted basis, small caps outperformed large caps by a substantial margin. Numerically, small caps averaged about 14 percent a year for those seven years versus 7 percent for large caps. On an equal-weighted basis, the pattern is much the same: Small-cap returns are 28 percent compared with 22 percent for large caps.

Exhibit 2 shows the small- and large-cap outperformers in emerging markets. Most Latin American countries, except for Venezuela, outperformed in the small-cap category. Venezuela is a very restricted market. It adopted foreign exchange con-

trols a few years ago, and financially, it is about as risky as a market gets. Among the large-cap outperformers is India, which is also a very restricted market. Foreigners can buy only through funds or Global Depositary Receipts, which sell at high premiums, or they can register to set up in India itself, a process that can take a substantial amount of time. Korea's limits on foreign ownership in stocks recently rose from 18 percent to 20 percent. Thailand also restricts foreign ownership, but at a slightly different level for each stock.

In summary, the data show that a small-cap effect does exist, even though the information is somewhat hard to find.

CURRENT DEVELOPMENTS

Small-cap investments are slowly beginning to become an asset class internationally, much as they are in the United States. The potential market size for capitalizations of less than $800 million is about $1.5 trillion. The float (stocks available for trading) is about 40 percent, or about $600 billion, which is a sizable amount of tradable assets, large enough to constitute a separate asset class in international small-cap stocks.

Table 2. Average U.S. Dollar Returns in Developed Markets

Date	Large Cap	Small Cap	Total
Capitalization weighted			
1989	6.755%	24.893%	12.604%
1990	–25.523	–24.688	–25.253
1991	8.960	5.349	7.798
1992	–14.971	–16.853	–15.579
1993	27.679	28.698	28.009
1994	8.378	12.554	9.723
1995	9.882	3.630	2.843
Cumulative total	11.942	23.679	16.021
Annualized	1.625%	3.083%	2.146%
Equal weighted			
1989	30.475%	31.914%	30.695%
1990	–12.953	–14.644	–13.517
1991	9.285	8.149	9.041
1992	–12.524	–9.156	–11.425
1993	36.263	42.829	38.361
1994	4.765	7.598	5.669
1995	18.339	13.937	16.959
Cumulative total	83.423	93.701	86.674
Annualized	9.053%	9.905%	9.327%

Note: The large-cap universe represents the largest 67 percent of each country's total market capitalization. The small-cap universe is composed of those companies falling between the 67th and 95th percentiles of each country's total market capitalization.

Source: Wilshire Associates.

Table 3. U.S. Dollar Returns in Emerging Markets

Date	Large Cap	Small Cap	Total
Capitalization weighted			
1989	39.840%	70.856%	50.072%
1990	−25.095	−22.399	−24.205
1991	13.699	20.571	15.943
1992	−7.230	0.725	−4.670
1993	55.408	69.109	59.947
1994	4.310	6.375	4.986
1995	−9.140	−13.375	−10.540
Cumulative total	62.734	150.913	88.864
Annualized	7.204%	14.045%	9.509%
Equal weighted			
1989	47.317%	58.924%	51.166%
1990	31.301	42.300	34.923
1991	47.835	55.756	50.931
1992	−9.534	3.788	−4.912
1993	58.981	62.330	60.402
1994	7.276	12.604	9.034
1995	−9.486	−12.817	10.688
Cumulative total	299.343	482.605	357.224
Annualized	21.873%	28.629%	24.252%

Note: The large-cap universe represents the largest 67 percent of each country's total market capitalization. The small-cap universe is composed of those companies falling between the 67th and 95th percentiles of each country's total market capitalization.
Source: Wilshire Associates.

Figure 1 shows regional mandates for 1991 through 1995. During the past five years, the international small-cap market has gone from zero to about $8 billion in U.S. tax-exempt assets alone. An average annual growth rate of 25 percent is forecast for the next five years, which could increase total international small-cap mandates to about $24 billion by the year 2000.

New indexes for the international small-cap category are being developed all the time, but none of the current ones is satisfactory. The index published by the Quantitative Techniques Division of HSBC James Capel, the HSBC James Capel World excluding U.S. Smaller Companies Index, is not bad, but it does not include the emerging markets. The capitalization of the Capel index is about $340 billion, which covers 1,200 firms with market caps between $150 million and $500 million.

Exhibit 1. Outperforming Developed Countries

Small Cap	Large Cap
Australia	Canada
Austria	Denmark
Belgium	Hong Kong
Finland	Ireland
France	Italy
Germany	Norway
Japan	Spain
Netherlands	Switzerland
New Zealand	United Kingdom
Singapore	
Sweden	

Source: Wilshire Associates.

The problem with some of these indexes is that they can be very skewed. The United Kingdom, for example, is weighted about 20 percent in the Capel index, which I believe overemphasizes a market that may not be that important. Salomon Brothers has also developed an index for international small-caps, but it is heavily weighted in Japan.

Exhibit 2. Outperforming Emerging Markets

Small Cap	Large Cap
Argentina	Greece
Brazil	India
Chile	Jordan
Colombia	Korea
Malaysia	Portugal
Mexico	Thailand
Nigeria	Venezuela
Pakistan	
Philippines	
South Africa	
Taiwan	
Turkey	
Zimbabwe	

Source: Wilshire Associates.

Much like small caps in the United States, the growth of emerging markets has been demand driven. Emerging markets have always existed, but they developed as an asset class only after information flows improved in the late 1980s. Investors wanted investments in emerging markets, and emerging market funds started to form, which allowed supply to develop as companies started issuing equity.

Figure 1. Small-Cap Mandates by Region

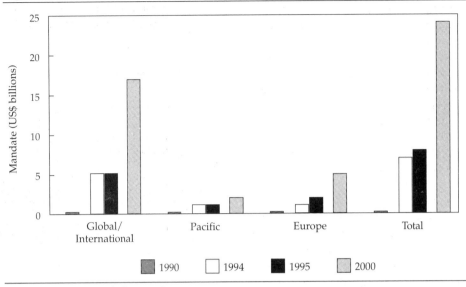

Source: InterSec Research Corporation.

More initial public offerings, secondaries, and rights issues are coming from small companies overseas as they try to fill demand for small-cap securities. Much of this demand is from U.S. mutual funds.

INTERNATIONAL SMALL-CAP INVESTING

Despite their weak performance in 1995, small-cap stocks gained strength in 1996. The Capel index is up about 10 percent through June, compared with 3.7 percent for the MSCI EAFE Index.

Attractions of Small-Cap Investing

Clearly, the major attraction of small-cap stocks is the historical evidence that they have outperformed larger stocks on a risk-adjusted basis. Low correlations with other asset classes also make international small-caps a good diversification tool. In addition, the small-cap market is still fairly inefficient and has less competition than most other asset markets. This combination of circumstances provides opportunities for investors who can get ahead on the learning curve, but investing in these markets ahead of the competition is getting harder to do.

International small-cap firms offer more growth opportunities in newer industries than do larger companies. An example is the predominance of small, new-technology companies in the United States. New companies start small, so by definition, that is where the real opportunities exist.

The new international small-cap indexes will permit easier benchmarking of investment performance. Morgan Stanley & Company is supposedly working on an index that could be ready shortly. That index will give credibility to investing in international small-cap stocks and attract a lot of money into the asset class.

Small caps are also relatively cheap, largely because they do not have much liquidity and investors tend to avoid them. In this case, illiquidity can actually be your friend, especially if you are a small money manager. If for some reason liquidity changes, then the stocks do very well. For example, a reduction of state or government ownership of small companies can dramatically change the value of those stocks as liquidity is provided. Getting in before that happens usually provides a good opportunity.

Most large-cap stocks have already been discovered and fairly valued. We have had a bull market for several years, so values, if they exist, are primarily in the small-cap firms.

Complexities of Small-Cap Investing

Investing in international small-cap stock clearly presents many difficulties. A major difficulty is the high cost of exiting positions that is caused by illiquidity, especially when foreign investors have constraints imposed on their investing activities. Another difficulty with investing in international small-cap stocks is lack of information. Often, no analysts follow a foreign small-cap company.

Some countries still have a lot of family or state ownership, so investing can be difficult for outsiders. Another problem is poor management. The quality of management overseas generally is not as good as in the United States, and that situation is exacerbated in small-cap companies. Investors have to be careful of whom they deal with. Our firm believes in quality, particularly in emerging markets. We want good companies, good management, good products, and good market share.

Another difficulty with international small-cap stocks at present is the inability to use an indexing strategy. Indexing is difficult because of illiquidity and transaction costs.

A VALUATION METHODOLOGY

Our firm's investing is based upon three themes. One is low valuation; some stocks are obviously undervalued. The second theme is growth at the right price. We are willing to pay more if we have a high degree of confidence in the earnings projections. Third is turnarounds; they can be undervalued, but they are not as evident as the other two attributes. For example, the P/Es might be sky high because the company's earnings have disappeared. We look for companies that might have had margins of 10 percent that then went to 1 percent but we think will go to 10 percent again. We are not contrarians. For a lot of stocks with a decline in earnings, their earnings keep on going down and never recover. So, we do a lot of analysis to see whether we think the company has recovery potential.

We are essentially stock pickers, so our process is dominated by a bottom-up approach. The bottom-up approach does not exclude macro factors, such as country dynamics, but we look first for companies that are the most undervalued and have the most appreciation potential. When looking at those companies, however, you also have to look at the country and the industry, because the growth rate of the country can affect, for example, the growth rate of earnings. Country factors also affect confidence in the earnings forecast. A potential currency devaluation or irregular economic growth can affect how a company performs. We factor all those variables into our earnings and cash flow analyses and use the country factors in our valuation models. We are very much value driven and use fundamental analysis to forecast earnings and cash flows, for instance, three to five years in the future.

Figure 2 compares the allocation of our portfolio with those of other managers and of the EAFE Index. The country weightings in EAFE are 40 percent in Japan, 16 percent in the United Kingdom, 6.5 percent in France, 6.8 percent in Germany, and 5.8 percent in Switzerland. The top five countries are about 80 percent of the EAFE—it is not well diversified. In the median weighting for the Frank Russell Company universe of international managers, the rank order of countries is about the same as in the EAFE. The top five holdings for the Frank Russell manager medians are 60 percent of the total.

The top five holdings for our firm are only 40 percent of the total, so we are more diversified than the indexes. The countries are very different from those of the major indexes, except for Japan, but we are only 9 percent Japan, whereas the Frank Russell

Figure 2. Five Largest Country Exposures: EAFE, Frank Russell Managers' Medians, and Jacobs Asset Management, June 30, 1996

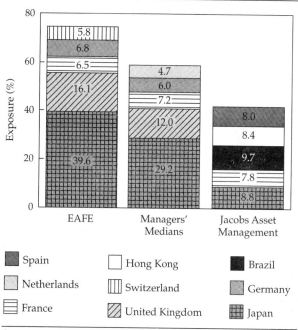

Sources: Jacobs Asset Management; Frank Russell Company.

universe is 30 percent and the EAFE Index is 40 percent. For France, we are about the same, but our weights for some other countries—Brazil, Hong Kong, and Spain—are totally different from those in the indexes. Again, our approach is stock picking, and it is very different from indexing.

To be an international investor, you should also be a U.S. investor. A global investor is well postured to do international investing, because many of the technology trends or new types of industries start first in the United States. Investors familiar with investing in those types of stocks or trends in the United States can apply that knowledge to overseas markets where those trends are starting and do better than somebody who is focusing only on Europe or on Asia. Industry familiarity is an advantage for investors who have a global perspective.

CONCLUSION

An international small-cap effect does exist, and as more people start to believe in it, international small caps are growing as an asset class.

Now is a good time to invest in international small-cap stocks, partly because large caps are generally fully valued. More importantly, most of the inefficiencies and undervaluation are in small caps.

Question and Answer Session

Daniel L. Jacobs, CFA

Question: Do you invest at all in Eastern Europe?

Jacobs: We do invest in that region, but because Eastern Europe is a fairly risky market, our investments tend to be in larger cap securities. The small-cap markets have not developed well yet in those areas.

Question: What are the good sources of information on countries?

Jacobs: We like to travel a lot and meet overseas managers and research analysts. We have very good overseas contacts, and we rely on them to be our network and our research staff. We also have all the best software and hardware for doing international research. Although we do screen, we mostly use our own knowledge and experience.

Question: What sources do you use to keep up with changes and differences in the accounting practices among countries? How do you normalize them across different countries?

Jacobs: Accounting practices do not change frequently. We try to keep up the best we can and to factor accounting differences into our analysis to allow comparison on an apples-to-apples basis. In such countries as Germany, we look at cash flow more than earnings; in other countries, we might look at enterprise value to earnings before interest, taxes, depreciation, and amortization. In such places as Mexico, where earnings are very volatile because of monetary corrections for inflation and foreign exchange gains and losses, we try to

do the best we can.

Our approach also provides opportunity, because the more inefficient these markets are, the harder it is to discern what the true value is and the greater the opportunity. That was particularly the case in international assets investing in the 1980s, but in the 1990s, information flows are better.

Question: Do you use economic data and top-down analysis to make decisions about where to invest in the emerging markets?

Jacobs: My main focus is to look for undervalued stocks, but when analyzing the stocks, I take macro factors, such as the stability of the country, into account. A stock's potential valuation might be less for Brazil than for Germany, for instance. The process is very subjective and judgmental, and it really depends heavily on how much confidence we have in our projections. Constantly trying to change our earnings projections because of what we think the country might do would unnecessarily bog us down. So, I merely project a company's earnings and cash flows for five years and then incorporate the country factors into the valuation process.

Question: Wal-Mart Stores is an example of a U.S. company expanding overseas. Are you finding a lot of other established companies moving into emerging markets?

Jacobs: The international portion of Wal-Mart's operations are still a small part of its business, but it takes time to build businesses in Brazil and Mexico, for instance.

Success requires good partnerships in the other country. Eventually, such moves will work for Wal-Mart, maybe not in 1996 but probably in two to three years. Many companies, such as Procter & Gamble, are overseas, but I do not see any noticeable trends at the moment.

Question: Do you hedge currency risk?

Jacobs: No, we do not, mainly because no one has proven that currency movements can be predicted consistently over short periods of time. Instead, we try to pick stocks. If we think that on a long-term basis, the currency is away from its fair value, we might adjust the valuation models for that particular stock, which may mean less return potential and might keep us from buying it.

Question: Are there any countries where you consider the political risk too unacceptable to invest there?

Jacobs: Venezuela perhaps, but that does not mean that it is going into revolution or turmoil or anything like that. I simply do not like the system there. Russia is very dangerous, but potentially very rewarding, and we do invest there. I do not like India. It is not a very open economy. Although it has a lot of potential, it never seems to get its act together.

Question: What do your clients measure you against?

Jacobs: I don't yet have a good index for international small-cap investing. Usually, clients measure us against the EAFE or, for emerging markets, an emerging-markets-only index. Sometimes, I suggest they use a weighted average of 85 percent EAFE and 15 percent Morgan Stanley emerging markets index, because during the past seven years, I averaged about 15 percent a year in emerging markets.

Question: You used an $800 million market cap as the cutoff for international small cap. Would you use that same size range to define small-cap companies in emerging markets, or would it be higher or lower?

Jacobs: I chose that cutoff point based on data availability. The definition depends on how much money is being managed. If you are managing $1 billion or so in small-cap international, you might not want to go less than a float of $300 million or $400 million. Only in the newest emerging markets

would a company be considered large at $800 million. In Sri Lanka or Pakistan or Egypt, that amount would be large, but in Brazil or Mexico or Indonesia, it is medium sized.

Question: Do you believe there is local interest and support for small-cap stocks?

Jacobs: Historically, local interest in small-cap stocks in many emerging countries has been poor. Investors are more comfortable in domestic large caps, but that situation is starting to change now because foreign (mostly U.S. and U.K.) investors are starting to drive many small-cap markets.

Question: How do you feel about some of the sub-Saharan African markets—for example, the Ivory Coast, Ghana, and Zimbabwe?

Jacobs: Those markets are indeed emerging markets, but they are not quite for me at this time. Also, stocks in South Africa are not cheap at the moment. I invested there a few years ago, and the stocks did well after the country changed political leadership. Currently, the stocks are not cheap enough to compensate for the risk involved.

Question: Typically, small-cap analysts overseas are young and inexperienced. Can you get good advice from them?

Jacobs: Sometimes the right *advice* may not be available, but you can get the analysis. I develop what I think are the best contacts, and that takes a lot of time. Most young analysts are average, but some of them are exceptional. If you can find the exceptional ones for each industry or each country, then you can do very well.

Optimal Fund Size and Maximizing Returns

John C. Bogle, Jr., CFA
Managing Director
Numeric Investors Limited Partnership

The total amount of assets under management by any one investment manager is relevant to the costs of trading and, hence, the size of returns. The optimal amount of assets managed may differ between manager and client: The smaller the asset pool, the greater the clients' returns but the smaller the manager's fee income. Performance-based fees offer a compromise solution.

Virtually the entire money management industry acts as though bigger is always better, striving to take on assets almost without limit. The idea of limiting asset growth is anathema to an industry driven more by the desire to be the biggest than a desire to be the best. This attitude is reflected by a recent *Wall Street Journal* article (September 24, 1996) describing a proxy statement by a mutual fund asking its shareholders to vote for a new 12b-1 fee. The money, it was argued, would be used to market the fund, the implication being that a larger fund would benefit shareholders through higher returns.

Do larger funds generate higher returns? Very little research has been done on the relationship between fund size and the returns the fund generates on those invested assets. I contend that managing a small pool of assets is preferable to managing a large pool, and the small pool is especially important in small-cap stocks, for which liquidity is more limited than for larger stocks.

SIZE AND COSTS

The insights for the relationship between size of holdings and transaction costs are based on an article by André Perold and Robert Salomon ("The Right Amount of Assets under Management," *Financial Analysts Journal*, May/June 1991:31–39). The concept is simply to maximize the amount of dollar wealth from the investment process by considering the diseconomies of scale associated with trading large positions and the adverse impact of large trades on trading costs.

The general theory is that costs rise as demand increases. This relationship is generally true, especially in the investment world. Commissions and bid–ask spreads increase, not disproportionately but relative to the assets being traded. The costs associated with the adverse price impact of a trade, however, increase rapidly. Obviously, the more you want to buy of a stock, the less willing the market is going to be to sell it to you, the greater the price concession you are going to have to bear, and the more the price will move. Opportunity cost, or the amount by which a price moves before you are able to purchase the security, also increases rapidly.

This trading effect is not uniform across the market. It varies with style. Momentum trades are liquidity-demanding trades, and their cost increases more than other trades over time. Value trades, in contrast, are liquidity-providing trades. Over time, they tend to cost less than momentum trades. Large-cap stocks have much more liquidity than small-cap stocks, so large-cap stocks are easier to trade. Index funds, of course, are less affected by a lack of liquidity, because they do not turn over rapidly—turnover for the S&P 500 Index, for example, is 3–5 percent a year. The important point is that, whether the trade is value or momentum, large or small, costs always rise as the amount of an asset traded increases, and this increase in costs has an adverse impact on total returns.

MEASUREMENT OF TRADING COSTS

Numeric's analysis of trading costs is performed by calculating how much the average execution price differs from the price of a security at the time it was identified as a buy. **Figure 1** presents a schematic in which a stock is identified as a buy at price A. The eventual trade, however, could occur at any price between A and B, or higher. This difference is the price impact associated with trade size. For larger trades, the eventual trade would occur closer to B, and for smaller trades, closer to A. The bottom line is that the greater the amount of shares to be traded,

Figure 1. Measurement of Trading Costs

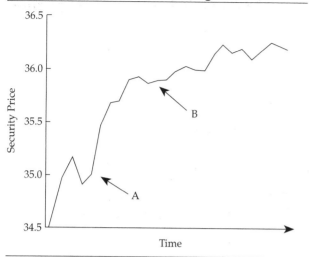

Source: Numeric.

the more the average execution price differs from A and the greater the transaction cost must necessarily be.

To understand how trading costs may be related to fund returns, we analyzed a total of about 10,000 transactions from October 1995 through July 1996 to study the impact of trade size on trading costs. The analysis ignores expenses for running a mutual fund, management fees, and so on. These expenses change the results slightly but not the conclusions.

Throughout the analysis, we used Numeric's small-cap growth strategy with about $350 million in assets under management, which is currently closed to new investment. The median market capitalization of stocks included in the study was about $800 million. Actual returns have been about 6 percent a year over the Russell 2500 growth index benchmark. The typical trade represents about 50 percent of the median daily trading volume of the stocks we are buying.

Figure 2 shows the breakdown of the actual cost of each trade classified by the fraction of a day's volume demanded of the market. For example, all the trades that represent less than one-eighth of a day's

Figure 2. Small-Growth Investment Strategy

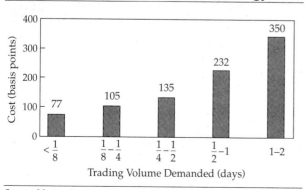

Source: Numeric.

volume (the leftmost bar) cost an average of 77 basis points (bps). This is a fairly high price impact for trades that do not demand a huge amount of liquidity from the marketplace. Trades that take between one-half and one day of volume cost about 232 bps. The greater the liquidity demanded, the longer the trading time required and the higher the cost of the trade.

At the current asset level, the demand on liquidity is between one-half to one full day, and total transaction costs for a one-way trade, according to our analysis, are about 184 bps. The total annual transaction costs can be calculated by multiplying average trading costs by the 300 percent turnover associated with this strategy and by a factor of 2 to account for both buy and sell transactions. The result equals 11 percent.

The theoretical return of the strategy is what that strategy would return if no transactions took place. The alpha of this theoretical or unencumbered strategy is 17 percent, which is calculated by adding the actual 6 percent return to the 11 percent in trade costs. Although 6 percent is a good return, it is much less than the theoretical return. Clients, however, would still earn more wealth than from an index strategy ($350 million times the 6 percent net return): a wealth generation of $21 million over and above the index.

What would happen if assets under management were doubled to $700 million? The results are shown in **Figure 3**. First, liquidity needs would double to one full day of trading because double the amount of assets under management would mean

Figure 3. Optimizing Wealth Generation

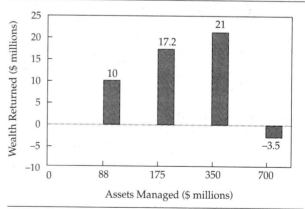

Source: Numeric.

trading twice as long for the typical trade. Trading costs would rise from 184 bps to 291 bps, and annual trade costs would rise to 17.5 percent. The total costs would be 291 bps times the 300 percent turnover times the factor of 2, or 17.5 percent. The net return here is the theoretical return of 17 percent minus the trading costs of 17.5 percent, or –0.5 percent. By doubling assets under management, the wealth *lost* by clients is the $700 million times –0.5 percent, or $3.5

million. Although the fund managers could have earned more fixed fees by doubling assets, their clients would lose $3.5 million.

If the amount of assets under management is reduced by half to $175 million, the typical trade time drops from one-half day to one-fourth day and the cost, according to our analysis, drops to 120 bps each way. Total trading costs are reduced to 7.2 percent: 120 bps transaction costs each way times 300 percent turnover times 2 for the two-way transactions. The alpha increases to the 17 percent theoretical return minus 7.2 percent transaction costs for a 9.8 percent return. Although the alpha in managing $175 million in assets is better than the alpha at $350 million, the absolute wealth clients earn is lower. We are able to return only $17.2 million in wealth to our clients (9.8 percent times $175 million). The returns are better, but are the clients really better off?

THE CONFLICT OF INTERESTS

The optimal amount of assets under management, from the manager's point of view, is a level just below the level at which returns start to become negative relative to the index. In the Figure 3 example, this optimum is near $700 million, where the manager is not likely to be fired for delivering near-index performance and management fees are maximized. Beyond this level, returns fall off and the manager probably starts to lose assets. The client, however, wants the manager to have as few assets as possible. Clearly, the compromise is somewhere between the two.

As is clear from this analysis, a conflict arises between the interests of the portfolio manager and the interests of the shareholder. The client wants assets minimized in order to maximize returns, but the manager wants to continue taking in assets to maximize the company's fees.

One way of resolving the issue is to impose performance fees. Client and manager interests are far better aligned if managers are paid on the basis of the wealth they generate. The typical performance fee pays managers a fixed percentage of the wealth returned. Sometimes, a modest base fee is charged. This system discourages managers from increasing assets at the expense of total return, is the best way to align the interests of the shareholders and the managers, and increases the shareholders' return.

CONCLUSION

Our research shows how and why trading costs eat away a greater portion of total returns as the size of assets managed increases. I believe this relationship between fund size and returns helps explain, in part, the mean reversion of excess returns that seems to be so prevalent in the asset management industry. Returns tend to be good for small funds, which allows a fund to profile its good returns in advertisements. This performance, in turn, attracts investors who invest too much capital in the fund. Trading costs go up, and eventually returns go down. Certainly, some funds do have good returns after they grow, but they tend to be the exceptions, not the rule.

This relationship also helps explain, I believe, the recent worsening record of active managers versus passive managers. As the assets managed by active investors have increased, their trading costs have increased, causing aggregate active management returns to be even lower than in the past, relative to passive managers.

The lack of interest by this industry in the relationship between size and returns is understandable, given the interests of the money management companies and the lack of awareness by investors. My hope and expectation is that investors will wake up to this issue and start to take the stand that bigger is not always better and that their interests are not always the same as the interests of the management company.

Question and Answer Session

John C. Bogle, Jr., CFA

Question: You say that reducing the size of assets under management is the best approach to preserving returns, but why not lower your turnover, because 300 percent may not be optimum?

Bogle: We have looked closely at the issue of turnover. Reducing turnover might cause us to hold on to securities for which the near-term returns may not be as good as returns for other opportunities. Our turnover at 300 percent turns out to be the optimal level for maximizing the amount of return we can generate for our investors.

Question: Do you adjust average daily volume for different exchanges, and if so, how?

Bogle: Yes, in this analysis, we have used the rule of thumb that the actual volume for Nasdaq trades is about 40 percent of the reported volume, to account for the double and sometimes triple printing.

Question: Do you use crossing networks for trading? What are the pros and cons?

Bogle: Yes, we do use crossing networks. We usually have more luck with them in our value-based trades that are contrarian in nature. The crossing networks have been dominated during the past few years by what we call the conventionals, which is traders like us who typically use momentum-based signals. Because so many traders using the electronic networks are on one side of the market, and often demanding large quantities of the same stocks, we have less success in trading the momentum-based positions.

We have always used the major crossing networks, but one day, the buys and the sells that we had left from the morning cross became mistakenly turned around so that buys became sells and sells became buys in the afternoon cross. Whereas our normal hit rate was probably something on the order of 2–3 percent of the names, the trades we put through hit about 30 percent of the trades that we had wanted, giving us a very clear indication that we were up against people who were looking at exactly the same stocks that we were.

Waiting for liquidity to show up in the electronic networks is not enough with momentum-based trades. One needs to go out and actively seek liquidity.

Question: In your analysis, you assumed that increased assets lead to higher trading costs because of liquidity demand. Couldn't you find other stocks that might not increase the liquidity problem, rather than increasing the purchase of existing companies?

Bogle: Although we do not optimize in the classic sense of portfolio optimization, we do optimize by finding the best liquidity available in the names we are trying to trade and the returns we are able to generate. In fact, for us to sacrifice those names and to look to alternatives would reduce returns modestly, net of trading costs.

Question: Do you return some of your investors' money when the fund grows too large?

Bogle: We have not yet been faced with that prospect. Instead, we shut the funds down when we think they are in danger of getting too large. We have shut down three of our investment strategies to new assets under management, and we are about to shut down a fourth. We have talked a number of times about the possibility of giving assets back. We went through this exercise to see if, in fact, our performance fees, meaning the wealth generated, would increase if we gave back assets under management. We are close enough to our peak that doing it made no sense, but we have considered it. At some point down the road, we probably will return investors' assets if the capital appreciation in these funds continues to outpace the increase in market liquidity.

Question: Once performance fees are introduced, clients typically want some compensation for underperforming years. How does your firm handle this issue?

Bogle: The SEC does not allow us to pay back fees. We structure performance fees that we believe are fair, about as fair as any we have seen. The way we structure performance fees for hedge portfolios is to have clients pay us a 1 percent base fee plus 20 percent of the amount we return to them over and above the Treasury bill return plus 1 percent. The performance fee is also structured on a from-inception basis. To the extent that performance is negative, we need to earn that back before we are able to pay ourselves any performance fee. Again, the performance fees are paid only after we have beaten our base management fee.

Question: Why not eliminate the problem associated with high transaction costs by using an indexing strategy?

Bogle: I agree that indexing has solid theoretical underpinnings. The average manager cannot consistently beat the index because the average manager is the index, so net of all fees and expenses, the average manager has to underperform the index. Some managers, however, perform good research, stay small, and manage portfolios aggressively. The difficulty, of course, is identifying them *ex ante*. Indexing and active management both have a place in this business.

The Size Effect: Evidence and Potential Explanations

Marc R. Reinganum
Director
Southern Methodist University Finance Institute

A size effect is apparent in return differentials between small- and large-cap stocks. Seasonality, beta, and transaction costs, alone, do not appear to cause this difference in return. Although the small-cap stock outperformance does not occur every year, some evidence indicates that it may be predictable.

In the late 1970s, when I was doing my initial work on small-cap stocks, the prevailing view was that markets are efficient: No one can beat the market, and the real benchmark is the market. My research, which indicated that over time, small-cap stocks seemed to do better than larger ones, was viewed with skepticism. Many researchers argued that I had misestimated risk or that I had not taken transaction costs into account—any type of error in the work that they could use to explain why my results on small-cap stocks were not reality.

In the mid-1980s, this view began to change. The small-firm effect, which was once considered a stock market anomaly, became mainstream. Soon, the investment and consultant communities began to break up the universe of securities into large cap, midcap, and small cap, realizing that for purposes of benchmarking, small caps were not directly comparable with large caps.

THE SIZE EFFECT

The size effect is the relationship among risk, return, and market capitalization. It is the empirical irregularity that over time, small-cap stocks outperform large-cap ones on a risk-adjusted basis. The size effect is a relative phenomenon, in that investors do not have to invest in the very small and illiquid stocks in the bottom decile to take advantage of the relationship between capitalization and return; even going from the largest cap category down to the next largest provides return improvements. The relationship is monotonic, although obviously, the biggest differences are observed between the two extremes.

To measure return differences by size, the first step is to create a size-based or decile portfolio for each year in the study period. For example, at the end of a given calendar year, the roughly 1,500 stocks traded on the NYSE are broken into 10 groups, with an equal number of securities in each group—the top 150 would form the large-cap portfolio, the bottom 150 would form the small-cap portfolio, and the others would be divided among the eight intermediate portfolios.

Figure 1 illustrates the size effect: the inverse relationship between market capitalization and return. The returns in each portfolio based on market caps are value weighted rather than equal weighted. On average, the smallest cap stocks have by far the largest returns and the largest cap stocks have the smallest returns.

Investors do not have to gravitate all the way to the smallest companies to get the benefits associated with smaller capitalization. Moving from the largest size category to the next largest, Portfolio 9, improves performance. **Table 1** demonstrates the magnitude of the difference. Over the 70-year period from 1926 through 1995, large-cap portfolios, on average, earned 11.5 percent a year. The smallest cap portfolios earned 22.6 percent—nearly double. By moving from Portfolio 10 to Portfolio 9, the average annual rate of return jumped from 11.5 to 13.2 percent, an increase of about 1.7 percent a year, which is not too shabby for most investors. Portfolio returns are very similar for Deciles 8 and 9; then there is a jump of about 200 basis points to Deciles 5, 6, and 7. Similarly, returns for Deciles 3 and 4 are nearly the same; 2 is slightly different from 3; and then the return leaps upward between Portfolio 2 and the very smallest portfolio.

Figure 1. Average Annual Returns of 10 Size-Based NYSE Portfolios, 1926–95

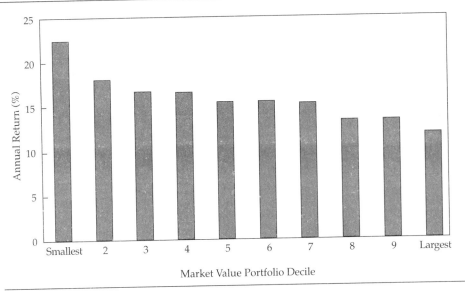

Source: Marc R. Reinganum.

Table 1 also lists the minimum and maximum annual portfolio returns over this 70-year period. When small-cap stocks pay off, they pay off big. For the largest cap portfolio, the best year's return in this 70-year period was 48.4 percent. For the smaller cap stocks, the best year was 225.9 percent. The payoffs are not symmetrical. The small caps may lose a little more in off years, but you cannot lose more than 100 percent. In their worst year, small-cap stocks lost 56.9 percent, and large-cap stocks lost 41.3 percent in their worst year. So, the performance differences are not tremendous on the downside, but they are very large on the upside.

EXPLANATION OF THE SIZE EFFECT

The size effect appears to have a strong seasonal component, with much of the overperformance concentrated in the month of January. **Figure 2** shows the annual return and the January return for the 10 decile portfolios. For the smallest cap stocks, the January return accounts for nearly half of the total annual performance. For Portfolio 2, the January return is a bit less than half of the total annual performance. For the largest cap portfolio, the January return is just about one-twelfth of the annual return.

Several explanations have been offered for the size effect. One is based on tax-loss selling. One way a company gets to be small cap is to have a substantial price decline. The tax-loss explanation argues that investors, for tax reasons, dump these stocks at the end of the year, thereby depressing the price. In January when this selling pressure disappears, the price bounces back, causing the observed abnormal returns in January. Research shows that, although some tax-loss selling may be going on, it cannot plausibly explain the entire January effect because

Table 1. Return Characteristics of the 10 Size-Based NYSE Portfolios, 1926–95
(percentages)

Decile	Average Annual Portfolio Return	Minimum Annual Portfolio Return	Maximum Annual Portfolio Return	Standard Deviation of Annual Returns
Smallest	22.61	–56.86	225.95	44.99
2	18.26	–51.42	139.02	35.76
3	16.79	–52.67	117.64	31.88
4	16.62	–47.15	112.82	30.94
5	15.51	–49.25	109.90	27.93
6	15.44	–47.04	108.33	27.70
7	15.27	–43.78	117.71	26.97
8	13.29	–48.79	85.45	23.09
9	13.24	–49.63	72.80	21.92
Largest	11.49	–41.33	48.42	18.85

Source: Marc R. Reinganum.

Figure 2. January and Entire-Year Average Returns, 1926–95

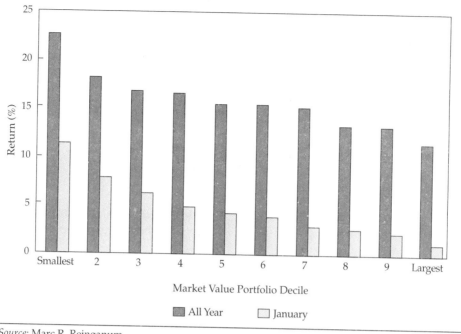

Source: Marc R. Reinganum.

stocks that are not likely to be sold for tax reasons also go up in value in January.

Another explanation for the small-cap January effect is based on the notion of information release—that in January, uncertainty about information gets resolved after the fiscal year-end, leading to a spike in prices. Although two-thirds of the companies listed on the NYSE have December fiscal year-ends, one-third of them do not. If the information-release hypothesis were true, then the June fiscal year-end companies would have a July effect, which they do not.

Still another explanation offered for the small-cap effect is differences in beta between the large- and small-cap stocks. This suggestion was the pet peeve of many researchers because the existence of a size effect would destroy the capital asset pricing model (CAPM) as a good empirical representation of the way the world works. The problem is that the data do not conform with the model.

One criticism of the evidence is that risk is misestimated because of such issues as nontrading. Even estimating risk in more appropriate ways than the original, naive methods used in earlier research does not help. **Table 2** shows CAPM risk parameter estimates: betas based upon annual returns. Issues of nontrading are not critical. Large firms have lower betas than small firms; that is, they are less risky than small firms. The question is: Are the differences in beta enough to explain the differences in returns? The large-cap companies had average annual returns of about 11 percent, the smallest cap companies had average annual returns of 22 percent, but the differ-

ences in beta are not large enough to explain the differences in return.

To illustrate why differences in beta do not explain differences in return, Table 2 also shows the implied market risk premium calculated as the differences in annual return divided by the differences in beta. The largest cap portfolio, which does not have an implied market risk premium, is used as the benchmark. All of the implied market risk premiums run between 12 percent and 14 percent—much greater than actual risk premiums. Even comparing the largest portfolio with Portfolio 9 yields about the same implied market risk premium as comparing the largest portfolio with the smallest.

Table 2. Portfolio Risk Characteristics of the 10 NYSE Size Portfolios, 1926–95

Decile	Estimated Portfolio Beta	Implied Market Risk Premium (%)
Smallest	1.71	14.62
2	1.50	12.30
3	1.37	12.65
4	1.37	12.31
5	1.25	13.27
6	1.27	12.46
7	1.25	12.59
8	1.09	12.48
9	1.07	14.33
Largest	0.95	na

na = not applicable.

Source: Marc R. Reinganum.

Potential transaction costs also might explain the differences in return between large- and small-cap stocks. Small-cap companies have lower priced stocks. As of June 30, 1996, on a cap-weighted basis, the small-cap stocks had an average price of about $10 a share; large-cap stocks had a price of $63. Even in the smaller categories, transaction costs are not a likely explanation for the size effect. Investors' true costs depend upon how long they hold the stocks, not just the stated spread. Calculated on an amortized basis, the spread would be between 0.5 percent and 1.7 percent. So, total transaction costs for small-cap stocks, including commissions, would be in the range of 1–2 percent, which is not enough to make the size effect go away.

How can one explain the substantial cross-sectional size variation in firms' performance? **Table 3** may provide some answers to why small-firm portfolios do better. About 10 percent of small firms double in value in a given year. In contrast, less than 1 percent of large-cap companies double their value in a given calendar year. A small-cap company is about 100 times more likely than a large-cap company to triple in value in a given year. The odds that a small-cap company will quadruple in value in a calendar year are about 1 in 100, but during the 70-year study period, no large-cap company quadrupled in value in one year.

FUTURE ISSUES

Although small-cap stocks, on average, outperform large-cap stocks, that is certainly not the case for every year. The question is whether these cycles of overperformance are predictable or occur at random. Certainly, given the notions of random walks and efficient markets, the a priori answer would be no. But it is important to beware of hubris and not blind oneself to potential opportunities. The variation in comparative performance appears to be predictable.

The time-series performance differential between small- and large-cap stocks appears predictable. The prediction is based in part upon return reversals and in part upon other economic and statistical variables. **Figure 3** shows the annual return differential for small- and large-cap portfolios. The difference in performance was clearly more pronounced in the 1930s than it has been recently. In some years, small-cap stocks do well, and in some years, they do poorly relative to large-cap stocks. The average difference between the two is about 11 percent, but the variability is substantial. In the 1970s and 1980s, small caps did well, but not so in the late 1980s and the early 1990s.

Figure 3. Differential Returns between Smallest and Largest Cap Portfolios

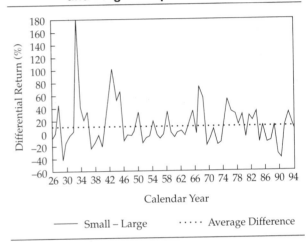

Source: Marc R. Reinganum.

Return reversals in stock returns have been well documented in the academic literature. This phenomenon is one in which the prior year's winners become the losers and the prior year's losers become

Table 3. Growth in Values for the 10 Size-Based NYSE Stock Portfolios, 1926–95
(percentages)

Decile	Firms That at Least Doubled in a Calendar Year	Firms That at Least Tripled in a Calendar Year	Firms That at Least Quadrupled in a Calendar Year
Smallest	10.25	2.87	1.12
2	7.05	1.15	0.40
3	5.92	0.84	0.26
4	5.22	0.78	0.20
5	4.10	0.49	0.16
6	3.78	0.42	0.11
7	3.05	0.41	0.09
8	2.54	0.25	0.04
9	1.80	0.16	0.03
Largest	0.89	0.03	0.00

Source: Marc R. Reinganum.

the winners. **Table 4** presents the autocorrelations of five-year differential returns between the small- and large-cap stocks. The autocorrelations measure the extent to which a five-year return is correlated with the return over the next five-year period. The autocorrelations are all negative, indicating the presence of a pattern of return reversals. The reversal pattern suggests that if small-cap stocks did very poorly in the last half of the 1980s, they would do well in the first half of the 1990s, which turned out to be correct. **Figure 4** shows five-year periods in which small-cap stocks underperformed large-cap ones, along with the last year of the subsequent five-year period. The results show that when small-cap stocks substantially underperform large-cap stocks (on a five-year horizon), small-cap stocks almost always rebound in the subsequent five-year period.

CONCLUSION

Overall, the size effect states that, on average and over long periods of time, small firms outperform large ones. This phenomenon does not occur every year, however. There is evidence now to suggest that periods in which small-caps are likely to over- and underperform are predictable. This attribute can help money managers plan portfolio allocations to the large-cap, midcap, and small-cap asset classes.

Table 4. Autocorrelations of Five-Year Differential Returns between Largest Cap Portfolio and the Other Nine Portfolios

Decile	Autocorrelation
Smallest	–0.34
2	–0.37
3	–0.37
4	–0.40
5	–0.38
6	–0.36
7	–0.44
8	–0.40
9	–0.49

Source: Marc R. Reinganum.

Figure 4. Differential Returns in Five-Year Periods following Superior Performance of Large-Cap Stocks

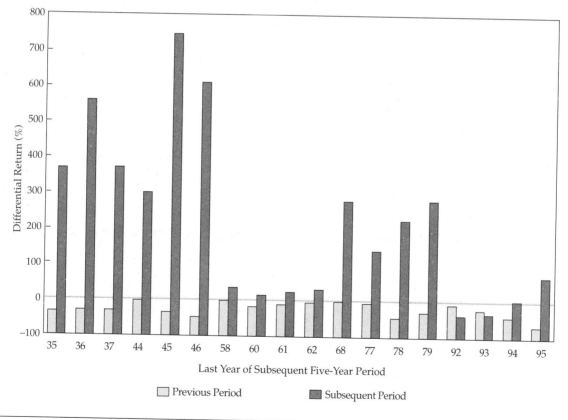

Source: Marc R. Reinganum.

Question and Answer Session

Marc R. Reinganum

Question: How much of the small-cap effect is attributable to the original cheapness of the stocks?

Reinganum: The smaller cap stocks do tend to be lower priced stocks. A company can fall into the small-cap category in at least two ways: Either it truly is a small, growth company that is just starting off, or it was a much larger company that fell on bad times. Size is measured by price times shares outstanding, and if the price has had a substantial decline, the company will be smaller than it was.

Question: Are the returns you show based on a particular trade size? Doesn't execution price differ according to the size of the trade?

Reinganum: Historical numbers are typically based upon end-of-day closing prices, which give no sense of how much depth is present at that price. That information is not given in the database. We are beginning now to collect volume statistics so we can assess depth at various prices. Obviously, 100 shares are a lot easier to place than 50,000 shares, especially in some small-cap issues.

Question: What is the impact of trading costs and liquidity on some of these analyses of small-cap performance?

Reinganum: Several academic papers have been written on this topic, and depending upon whose you read, some have negated the fact that a small-cap effect exists. Others support the notion that,

even taking the transaction costs into account, small caps carry some premium. The answer depends on how the studies are structured. Theory suggests that prices normally change in response to new information, not to liquidity trades.

Question: Small companies grow a lot faster when they are still small. Is part of the explanation for the small-cap effect related to small-company fundamentals as opposed to large-company fundamentals?

Reinganum: Growth companies are not the only type of small company that does well. Small companies with terrible earnings growth also do well. A company may have terrible news, been beaten down, and then come back up. It would be a mistake to infer that small-cap performance is being driven exclusively by these rising stocks, because that is not the case.

Question: How would your results be different if your universe also included OTC stocks? I know that the data do not go back to 1926.

Reinganum: The larger sample would be similar but not identical to the NYSE sample. I have examined this issue and found that the results using Nasdaq stocks are much the same but with some differences. Over the time period I studied, the small NYSE stocks had slightly higher returns than similar-sized Nasdaq stocks. My explanation for it was that, in part, returns reflect not only risk but also

liquidity premiums. I argued that the small-cap companies compete more to provide liquidity services on the Nasdaq than on the NYSE.

Question: What effect do initial public offerings and the "IPO pop" have on the small-firm effect?

Reinganum: The IPO pop is a drag, not a pop. The empirical evidence suggests that over time, IPOs underperform, not outperform. Look at the difference since June 1996 between the Russell 3000 Index and the S&P 500 Index small caps. The IPOs in the Russell these days have been a real drag on its return.

Question: Might family-controlled businesses have any impact on the small-cap effect? Some research suggests that family-controlled businesses have outperformed in the long run because of how they are controlled.

Reinganum: The question of the effect of family control gets to the issue of ownership, the structure of ownership, and how the structure of ownership affects performance. Research has shown that the more closely aligned the interests of the manager with the interests of the shareholders, the better it is for shareholder value. So, closely held firms should do pretty well. Other studies, however, have looked at the deaths of CEOs and principal shareholders in smaller companies; when the CEO and founder dies, the stock tends to pop up in value. So, the effect of family ownership may not necessarily be a positive influence for companies.

Self-Evaluation Examination

1. The size effect is:
   a. The relationship among risk, return, and market capitalization.
   b. An empirical irregularity that over time, large-cap stocks outperform small-cap stocks on a risk-adjusted basis.
   c. An empirical irregularity that persists year in and year out.
   d. An empirical irregularity that cannot be captured in an investment strategy.

2. Reinganum offers which of the following explanations for the size effect?
   a. The size effect is based on tax-loss selling.
   b. The size effect is based on the notion of information release.
   c. The size effect is based on differences in beta between the small- and large-cap stocks.
   d. All of the above.

3. According to Koenig, investors in microcap securities should look for all of the following *except*:
   a. Unlimited potential.
   b. Blue-chip capability.
   c. Popular sectors.
   d. Solid management team.

4. The research function in the small- and microcap sectors is very similar to that for large-cap securities.
   a. True.
   b. False.

5. For active small-cap managers, the greatest limitation is:
   a. The number of companies that can be owned.
   b. Adequate diversification.
   c. Transaction costs.
   d. The number of attractive stocks.

6. According to Bogle, in the money management business:
   a. Bigger is always better.
   b. Bigger is never better.
   c. Bigger is better up to a point.
   d. Size is not a factor in determining success.

7. Reilly lists three key elements to the buy decision:
   a. High growth rates, strong value characteristics, sparse Wall Street following.
   b. Above-average growth rates, strong value characteristics, sparse Wall Street following.
   c. High growth rates, strong value characteristics, moderate Wall Street following.
   d. Above-average growth rates, strong value characteristics, moderate Wall Street following.

8. The major disadvantage of using the Russell 2000 as a benchmark is:
   a. It has a high turnover rate.
   b. It has an average market cap of about $500 million.
   c. It has a low turnover rate.
   d. None of the above.

9. One of the difficulties in investing in international small-cap stocks is:
   a. The high cost of exit strategies.
   b. Lack of information.
   c. Poor management.
   d. All of the above.

10. A good investment process should include all of the following *except*:
    a. The generation of investment ideas.
    b. Qualitative research.
    c. Good sell-side analyst connections.
    d. A sell decision.

11. The data collection process is a critical part of quantitative analysis for small-cap stocks because:
    a. Clean and pertinent data are essential.
    b. Historical ticker numbers may not be consistent.
    c. Published data may not be accurate.
    d. All of the above.

Self-Evaluation Answers

1. a. The size effect is the relationship among risk, return, and market capitalization. The empirical irregularity is that small-cap stocks outperform large-cap stocks on a risk-adjusted basis over time. Although small-cap stocks outperform large-cap stocks on average, that is not the case for every year. According to Reinganum, the performance differential between small- and large-cap stocks appears predictable, and the number of investors using a small-cap strategy suggests that value can be captured.

2. d. All three of these have been offered as possible explanations for the size effect, but none is widely accepted as the explanation for the effect.

3. c. Koenig lists four things to look for in picking microcap stocks: unlimited potential, success recognition, blue-chip capability, and solid management. He believes investors should avoid over-populated sectors because there are so many firms in these areas that it is hard to know whether you have found the successful one.

4. b. As Schliemann discusses, the research function is very different. Relative to their larger counterparts, small firms must be analyzed in a more dynamic and higher risk environment.

5. a. As Schliemann discusses, the greatest limitation is the number of companies that can be owned, because it takes so many resources to follow small-cap companies.

6. c. Bogle argues that there is an optimal size. The optimal amount of assets under management from the manager's point of view is a level just below the level at which returns start to become negative relative to the index.

7. b. The Putnam approach is based on above-average growth rates, strong value characteristics, and sparse Wall Street following. Companies that are not actively covered will have small institutional ownership and thus provide a substantial opportunity.

8. a. Mott believes that the high turnover rate is a major disadvantage of the Russell 2000.

9. d. Jacobs describes how all of these characteristics can be problems when investing in international small-cap stocks.

10. c. As Breed notes, relying on a sell-side analyst is not prudent, because when news breaks, the analyst is not likely to call you first.

11. d. Ginsparg describes all of these potential problems and more in his discussion of using quantitative methods in managing small-cap portfolios.